FACTFINDER GUIDE

MYTHOLOGY

FACTFINDER GUIDE

MYTHOLOGY

Edited by Jo Forty

PRC

This edition first published in 1999 by
PRC Publishing Ltd,
Kiln House, 210 New Kings Road, London SW6 4NZ

ISBN 1 85648 540 5

Printed and bound in China

Previous pages, from left to right: Nike, Sakhmet, Romulus and, Remus, Zeus.

Right: Ascelpius.

CONTENTS

The ruins of the Temple of Apollo at Delphi.

INTRODUCTION

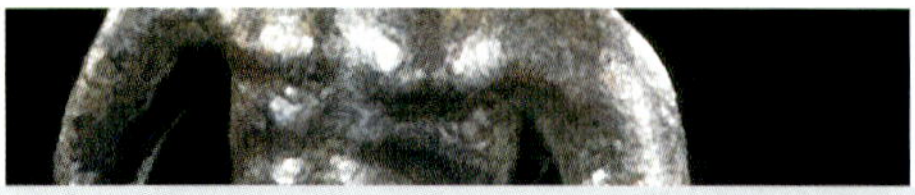

Introduction

"Throughout the inhabited world, in all times and under every circumstance, the myths of man have flourished; and they have been the living inspiration of whatever else may have appeared out of the activities of the human body and mind. It would not be too much to say that myth is the secret opening through which the inexhaustible energies of the cosmos pour into human cultural manifestation." (Joseph Campbell)

Heracles.

Mythology is intrinsic to humankind. All races without exception possess a mythology, and to study mythology at a worldwide level is to trace the pattern of humankind's spiritual, mental, and intellectual development. There has been no age nor civilization that has not probed the mysteries of life and attempted to explain them by the means of myth. The preoccupying questions have not fundamentally changed either—how was the world brought into being, what forces govern a person's life, and how best can he or she adapt to them and make them favorable to him or her? The answers have been as different and varied as the societies that have produced them.

At the beginning of this century, the view of Western rationalism concerning mythology was that myths were exclusive to primitive societies and had no place in modern civilization—which had evolved through reason and the burgeoning sciences away from such imaginative explanations. It was said that in more primitive times the world had been interpreted emotionally as a conflict of individual and inconsistent wills with which all phenomena were imbued by an imaginative and interactive humankind. At that time, even within Western society, religion was a much stronger part of everyday existence. Yet even now, the closer one looks into the origins of any modern nation, the more mythical it becomes. If this is the case,

Heracles killing the Nemean lion.

Isis suckling Horus.

then mythology is merely the term we use for cultural explanations alien to our own.

Freud and Jung both began to develop the modern understanding of mythology, linking it to our subconscious. Freud interpreted dreams and myths as being a reflection of our often thwarted or sublimated desires and needs. Jung saw myths as being a part of a collective unconscious that was shared by all humankind and contained the archetypes of our various evolutionary states. These combined to work our conscious minds through to new thresholds of transformation.

A more recent development is structural comparative mythology, as propounded by Levi-Strauss. This is a progression or continuation of Freud and Jung, and analyzes myths by breaking each one down into its constituent parts to reveal the structure of archetypes beneath. The structural mythologists believe that the basic idea behind most myths is the reconciliation of opposites in order to overcome the contradictions that naturally manifest in daily life. This is a process of "if you can conceive it, you can achieve it."

Nowadays, mythologists realize that all societies, no matter how ancient or contemporary, have their own mythologies, as integral as their own customs and fashions—all of which combine to form a contemporary matrix of factors that make each phase of time unique. Just as time moves forward, so these paradigm shifts are in a constant process of evolution. As older constructs fade, the warp and weft of our world changes and mutates. Have we now a burgeoning world mythology, or is it that almost all humankind's belief systems are currently operational, giving a truly spectacular breadth to our vision and imagination?

INTRODUCTION

Copy of the chryselephantine statue of Athena by Phidias.

Icon of the pharaoh: Horus wearing the Double Crown.

Achilles fighting.

All seek to explain and decode the world around us, and our own often contradictory drives and needs within it. The object of myth is to explain the world (as is the object of science); to make it more friendly and accessible to us. Yet one's belief is tempered by one's self knowledge and awareness—at both a personal and a social level. None of us individually know how to operate or function scientifically—science is merely the pooled use of cumulative data, a particular way of interpreting the world that falls far short of explaining its mystery. In reality, science is a kind of modern myth, with every fact merely a working hypothesis until augmented, corrected, or disproved by further advances or changes of thought. Also, within our own much larger and more complicated societies, in the absence of an effective general mythology, each of us has our "private, unrecognized, rudimentary, yet secretly potent pantheon of dream;" our own secret mythology. Being aware and at the center of our own existence, we are everything we believe ourselves to be, and perhaps a little more besides.

Over the millennia of humankind's historical culture, the stories have wended, mutated, and metamorphosed, carrying on irresistibly as time tracks forward. In spite of their beguiling diversity, they still resonate with an intrinsic similarity—a thread of continuity that runs through them all. Myths are made

Athens, the Acropolis and theatre of Herodias Atticus.

INTRODUCTION

Artemis, with one of her hounds.

to explain the world, to make sense of it, and to take possession of the world in conceptual symbolic forms in order to achieve a kind of physical possession too—a target bonding system of the desires and needs of our own individual selves and their external manifestation—societies. By explaining the world through stories, we overcome our fears and uncertainties, and attach meaning and logic to illogical things, slowly getting a grip on them. Also, myth appeals to the subconscious, intuitive world of feelings—impressions gained from all our senses and our cell awareness at a sub-vocal, intuitive level.

When myths finally are superseded, they are remodified or collected as stories with which to entertain ourselves, increase our knowledge, and gain new awareness. When old myths finally lose the meaning of their form, new ones are needed and made—the hybrids of a world culture in constant fusion. Based in reality they explain, illustrate, and justify. Where they are still implicitly believed, they live and are used to integrate and illustrate our thoughts and arguments, exorcise our demons, and inspire confidence, example, and reflection.

The clothing of mythology—gods, beasts, physical places—all are ciphers and symbols, avatars of intangibles that can manifest in new ways or remain almost eternally the same. A case of "the

Mount Olympus, the home of the Greek gods.

symbol restores the theme," and so conveys the sacred axiomatic truths of existence.

"It has always been the prime function of mythology and rite to supply the symbols that carry the human spirit forward, in counteraction to those other constant human fantasies that tend to tie it back. In fact it may well be that the very high incidence of neuroticism among ourselves follows from the decline among us of such spiritual aid." (Joseph Campbell)

The ancient Classical mythology of the Graeco-Roman period, with its Mesopotamian and Egyptian influences, is part of our ancient coda. Though not fully alive, like, say, those of India, these myths still have a cultural resonance and remain full of meaning and relevance. Look at any high art and culture in our present civilization—plays, theater, literature—and there they are. Many modern hybrids have an ancient kernel, too, because our basic nature has not changed and neither have our requirements. As well as Classical myths, we have our own modern mythology—(atomic) bomb culture, socialism and all the other -isms of progress, road movies, rock legends, gangster mythology, and sporting heroes—to help us make sense of the world. The modern electronic media together make a sophisticated machine for pumping these new myths up and out, into our conscious and subconscious.

The term "Classical Mythology" used in the title of this book covers a discernible geographic area and a specific time. This area spreads across the Mediterranean and combines with the Near and Middle East, and contains vir-

The original Sphinx at the Giza necropolis, Khufu's pyramid behind.

Amun-Re, paramount deity of the Egyptian pantheon.

tually the whole of the known Ancient World. The time covered spans from the growth of the first river-based civilizations in Mesopotamia and Egypt to the passing of the Old Gods from the Roman Empire and the advent of Christianity—some three and a half millennia. During this time firstly Sumer, Babylon, and Egypt, then Greece and her Roman inheritors adapted and absorbed the culture that each found in its turn, combining it in their own unique way to form a tradition or approach that has threads of continuity and syncretism that stretch down to Christianity and beyond.

Sumer and Egypt were two of the four great centers of early civilizations (China and the Indus Valley being the other two). Their achievements included working in stone and metals, design of a written language, and the development of cities. These cities were set in the alluvial plains of great rivers, their religions and protocols were concerned with the organization of the vital resource of water and its use in irrigation. Writing and other specialized occupations were the radical new steps of the first cities. City dwellers were often not directly involved with subsistence agriculture, but they helped to develop the technology to improve crop yields, and also traded any surplus. So began the development of hierarchical societies.

In Egypt, the Two Lands were held by one pharaoh when strong—a divine being who was worshipped as a manifestation of a god. In Mesopotamia, kingship was granted by the gods; the kings were the stewards of those gods who owned and controlled everything. Cities were based around a temple or holy area, and replacing and renewing these gradually led to a mound with

A Romanised Anubis.

A Roman silver platter with the head of Neptune.

The Lion gate at Mycenae.

walls built around it for protection. In Mesopotamia, mud bricks were used due to the scarcity of stone, which stimulated inventiveness and trade as well as new building techniques. Craftsman who made luxury items required raw materials, and the workshops in Mesopotamia and Egypt traded commodities and ideas, leading to a new phase in the development of human society. Their inheritors in turn continued this development, bequeathing to us, their descendants, a thread that links us back to the first civilizations. (Although mythology goes back much further and forward too—essential, intrinsic, vital, and inevitable.)

Originally, Mesopotamia consisted of independent city states that each had their time of prominence: Ur, Uruk, Eridu, Umma, Ebla, Mari, Adab, Nippur, Akshak, Sippar, Der, Nuzi, Nineveh, Akkad, Susa, and Babylon. Usually independent, they gradually linked together through alliance and conquest. Eventually they were all linked by the conquest of the upland Iranians. These cities were Temple and Palace bureaucracies, a feature in common with all early civilizations. Trade was vital, as Mesopotamia lacked all kinds of commodities. Many Hurrite and Hittite records have been found at Babylon, detailing the extent of trade and intimating the large size of the administration. Writing initially developed through the keeping of temple accounts and data concerning agricultural sewing and harvesting times (such as moon data). The earliest writing in the form of clay tablets was found at Uruk and dates from 3100 BC. It was made by marking the wet clay with the end of a reed stalk. A pictographic script then developed, and slowly changed into cuneiform. Literary compositions and poetry then followed. Sumerian culture and religion left its mark on all the proceeding religions.

Egypt, again, was river-born, perhaps with some initial Mesopotamian influence and trade, but, given its isolated geographical location, Egypt developed a distinct and original culture of its own. Its cities developed from cult centers, too, gradually combining in ever larger alliances until the Two Lands came into being. Its writing was also pictographic, and, thanks to the consistency of the Nile with its regular inundation of rich nutritious sediment, crop-growing was pioneered as well as transporting and working in stone. The Egyptians were also preoccupied with life after death, wishing to continue the heaven of life by the Nile through correct religious observance and protocol. Again, royal and religious hierarchies grew around these social advances.

Dorian Greece took from the original Minoan-Mycenaen civilization, which in its turn had traded and interacted with both Mesopotamia and Egypt.

Though Greece sneered at the East for its political stasis, in Ionia (Asia Minor) and Crete, and thence to the mainland, they took gods and myths, modifying them to suit their needs, as well as being influenced by the architecture and literature of the preceding civilizations.

With Rome, the emphasis drifts still further west, the European side of the Mediterranean gradually coming into prominence. The Romans were tolerant of all gods, accepting the transfer of older eastern deities, which combined with and modified their own. Perhaps more practical, they dealt in the reality of an immensely varied empire and attempted to secularize the state to a degree with an ever increasing judiciary and a growing body of laws.

FACTFINDER GUIDE:

The birth of Athena, springing fully armed from the head of Zeus.

MYTHOLOGY

A

ACHILLES

Perhaps the greatest figure in Greek mythology. It is around him that Homer's *Iliad* is woven: the tale of the wrath of Achilles is played out on the stage of the fall of Troy. His father was Peleus, king of Phthia in Thessaly, and his mother was Thetis, daughter of Oceanus. While still an infant, his mother plunged him into the River Styx that divided earth and Hades to ensure that he would be invulnerable to any weapon. In so doing, however, she retained hold of him by his heel, which would later be the cause of his downfall and the origin of the modern phrase for a person's weak spot—the "Achilles heel."

The ultimate Greek warrior: Achilles.

Thetis knew that Achilles would fall at Troy. He had the option of a short but glorious life if he went, or of a long inglorious existence if he did not. He was educated firstly by the Centaur **Chiron** and then Thetis tried to alter his fate by sending him away to the court of King Lycomedes, where he was disguised in female dress among the king's daughters. Wily **Odysseus**, knowing it was prophesied that Troy could not be taken without the help of Achilles, went in search of him. Gaining access to the women's quarters disguised as a peddler, he displayed his wares, having cunningly concealed fine weapons and a war trumpet among them. When Odysseus sounded the trumpet, Achilles immediately seized upon the weapons—thereby betraying himself—and then went off to the war with Odysseus. To safeguard her son, Thetis persuaded **Hephaestus**, the smith god, to make Achilles a suit of armor that was proof against any weapon.

In a division of spoils during the war, Achilles lost his favorite mistress, Briseis, to **Agamemnon**, and then refused to fight; instead he sat in his tent and sulked. With Achilles absent from the

Actaeon being attacked and consumed by his own hounds.

fray, the Trojans began to gain the upper hand, so Achilles' close friend, **Patroclus**, donned the armor of Achilles and went out to rally the Greeks. But Patroclus was killed by the Trojan prince, **Hector**, son of King **Priam**. This spurred Achilles to revenge and he killed Hector in single combat and then treated the corpse shamefully by dragging it around the walls of Troy behind his chariot. The gods condemned this treatment of the dead and forced Achilles to receive Priam, the grieving father, and restore the body to him for proper burial.

In the 10th and last year of the siege, **Paris**, another of Priam's sons, found Achilles in the temple of **Athena** courting Polyxena, his sister. Paris aimed an arrow at Achilles' heel, from which wound he died. There are countless stories of the deeds of Achilles in the *Iliad* and many others were invented and attributed to his name.

ACTAEON

A hunter and grandson of **Apollo** in Greek mythology, Actaeon was raised and taught to hunt by the Centaur, **Chiron**. One day, while out with his hounds, Actaeon chanced upon the virgin huntress-goddess **Artemis**, bathing naked in a pool accompanied by her maidens. Incensed by this intrusion, she changed Actaeon into a stag and set his own pack of hounds on him, who failed to recognize him and hunted him to his death. His discovery of the goddess and his dreadful end was a favorite subject for vase paintings in antiquity.

ADAD

Mesopotamian weather god, son of An (also sometimes of Nanna-Su'en). Portrayed in mythological and religious texts both as a bull and a lion, Adad embodies the violent thundering rainstorms that sweep the landscape of the Near East. In human form he is a warrior, riding his chariot harnessed to the storms across the sky. A common epithet for Adad is "Canal Inspector of Heaven and Earth," and he is involved with his brother **Shamash** in the administration of oracles. Adad has a temple in the city of Enegi near Ur, and in Babylon, and he also shared a temple with his father, An, in Assur, the capital of Assyria. His symbol is a forked lightning bolt.

ADAPA

One of the Seven Sages of Mesopotamian mythology, and the hero of Akkadian myth, which shares with the *Epic of* ***Gilgamesh*** the theme of man's failure to attain immortality. Adapa, a son of the god **Ea**, lived in the city of Eridu, where he carried out cultic duties. While fishing in his boat one day he was suddenly wrecked by the South Wind. In return Adapa broke the wing of the South Wind by means of a powerful spell. Anu, chief god of the pantheon, dispatched his vizier Ilabrat to summon Adapa to heaven to explain the absence of this wind. Ea, wishing to save Adapa's life, recommended that he don mourning garb to flatter the two gods who man the gate, and told him what to say. Above all he was to reject any offered hospitality. By following Ea's advice, Adapa safely negotiated Anu's questions and was later returned to earth, where his city received special favors but, by having refused food and drink at Anu's hand, he lost his chance for eternal life.

ADONIS

Although best-known from Greek legend, the roots of his myth are firmly based in the ancient Near East around Syria and the Lebanon, where there was a river named after him whose waters were reported to run blood red on the anniversary of his death. He was the son of Cinyras, king of Cyprus, himself a son of **Apollo**. Adonis' mother was Myrrah, who developed an unnatural passion for her father, Cinyras, and tricked him into an incestuous union. When he discovered the deception he attempted to kill her, but she fled to Arabia where, having given birth to Adonis, she was changed into a myrrh tree, giving it her name. **Aphrodite** loved the beautiful boy and gave him to **Persephone** to look after. Both goddesses were fond of him, especially Aphrodite as he grew into a handsome youth, and she warned her lover against his passion for hunting. He was eventually gored to death by a wild boar and the goddess' tears (in some versions Adonis' blood) dropped to earth and produced the blue anemone flower. Other legends say Aphrodite changed him into the flower after his death.

AENEAS

A Trojan prince, the son of Anchises by the goddess **Aphrodite** or **Venus**. The most valiant of the Trojan heroes at the siege of Troy, he was always to be found where the fighting was thickest. On several occasions, Aeneas was spirited away by various gods when he appeared hard-pressed, because they were mindful of a prophecy that said he

Aeneas.

would rule the Trojans, with his sons continuing as rulers. At the fall of Troy, Aeneas carried his aged father away on his back through the flames, together with his wife, Creusa, and son, Ascanbius. The scene was a favorite one for vase painters and also appeared on the coins of Julius Caesar (who claimed the Julian line to be descended from Venus via Aeneas). Subsequently he embarked on widespread travels, arriving in Sicily, where Anchises died and was buried. An adverse wind then blew Aeneas' ship to Carthage, where he was loved by **Dido**, its queen, who wished to marry him. This sojourn forms a major element in Roman poetry relating to Aeneas, especially that of Virgil where he is the protagonist of the great poem, the *Aeneid*. This was essentially a piece of propaganda for the Roman emperors' descent from the gods. Episodes from the *Aeneid* are common in Roman art, on all sorts of pottery and silver vessels, in painting, sculpture, and on mosaics.

Aeneas, leaving Dido and Carthage behind, eventually landed at the mouth of the Tiber (having first visited the famous Sibyl at Cumae, who showed him Hell). He was hospitably received by the local king, Latinus, and after several battles with rivals and enemies married Latinus' daughter, Lavinia, and succeeded Latinus as king. According to Roman tradition, Aeneas was drowned in the River Numicus in a battle against the Etruscans. His body was never found (probably due to the weight of his armor), but it was thought he had been taken up by the gods and duly offered sacrifices as one of their number. Tradition also gives him four sons—Ascanius, Euryleon, **Romulus**, and **Remus**—the third of whom was the eponymous founder of Rome. Thus Virgil, and the Latin poets who followed him, could produce a lineage for the Roman emperors that stretched back into prehistoric time and a relationship with the gods.

Golden deathmask from Mycenae, said to be of Agamemmnon.

AGAMEMNON

In Greek legend, king of Mycenae and Argos. His brother was **Menelaus**, king of Sparta. The brothers married two half-sisters, the daughters of **Leda**: **Clytemnestra** and **Helen**. Clytemnestra had previously been married to **Tantalus**, but Agamemnon killed both her husband and her infant son and married her. Her brothers, the **Dioscuri**, vowed vengeance but eventually agreed to make peace. The marriage was cursed from the start, however, as events were to show.

At the start of the Trojan War, Agamemnon was elected as the leader of the Greeks, the Acheans, and throughout it he showed great bravery. But a blight hung over the campaign because of his quarrels with **Achilles**, especially when he insisted in taking Achilles' mistress/slave Briseis, as part of his due. The "Anger of Achilles" in the ninth year of the siege was, in effect, the main theme of the *Iliad*.

After Troy had fallen by subterfuge (the Trojan Horse introduced armed men into the city who then opened the gates to the Greeks), Agamemnon received **Cassandra**, daughter of **Priam** and Hecuba, as part of his spoils. Cassandra prophesied that Agamemnon would be killed by his wife, but he chose to disregard her. At home in Mycenae, however, Clytemnestra had taken a lover, Aegisthus, and together they planned his murder. Accounts vary, but the most popular has it that when Agamemnon emerged from a bath Clytemnestra handed him a shirt with its sleeves sewn up. As he struggled to put it on she and her lover attacked him with axes and cut him down, also murdering Cassandra. The murder was a popular scene represented on Greek vase paintings. Agamemnon's son by Clytemnestra, **Orestes**, avenged his father by killing both the murderers, with the consequent charge of matricide being leveled against him.

AHURAMAZDA

Later called Ormuzd and principal deity in Zorastrianism, the religion of ancient Iran. This doctrine, propounded by Zarathustra (Zoroaster) and traditionally dated to 628–551 BC, entails a dualistic system of Good, created by Ahuramazda, opposed by Evil, embodied in Ahriman. Fire was central to Zoroastrianism, as is evident from the excavations of Sassanian fire temples and the recurrence of fire altars on Sassanian coins. It appears that the Achaemenid kings (the dynasty founded by Cyrus, 550–530 BC), may well have been Zoroastrians, since such rulers as Darius, Xerxes, and Cyrus describe Ahuramazda as the "greatest of all the gods" in their inscriptions, although without denying the power of other gods who find no mention in the Avestan literature. Ahuramazda is often considered to be represented in the characteristic winged disc containing a human figure found in Achaemenid sculpture, a device that itself derives from Assyrian representations of the national god Assur. Clear representations of Ahuramazda are found in scenes showing the investiture of the Sassanian kings.

AJAX

There are two heroes named Ajax in the Greek legends. To differentiate them they are often referred to as the Great and the Lesser Ajax; both served in the Trojan War, but the former was the greater and more pleasant character.

Ajax the Lesser was the son of Oileus, king of Locris. He was unpleasant in his manners and irreligious in his attitudes. The night Troy fell he pursued **Cassandra** to where she had taken sanctuary in the temple of **Athena**, clasping the cult statue. Ajax carried both her and the statue off and then raped the girl. Athena sought revenge for this impiety and destroyed his ship on the way home, but Ajax swam to a rock and boasted that he was safe despite all the gods. This was too much for them, particularly **Poseidon**, who with his trident smashed the rock to which Ajax clung causing him to drown. His impiety lived on after him when epidemics broke out in Locris and there were bad harvests. An oracle said that these misfortunes were the result of Athena's continued anger at the rape of Cassandra and the violation of her sanctuary. The Locrians were then told to send a pair of girls, chosen by lot, to Troy each year for a thousand years. This was done; the first two were killed by the Trojans, but subsequent victims—if they could escape the mob—spent the rest of their days, unmarried, in Athena's sanctuary.

Ajax and Achilles playing dice.

Ajax the Greater was the son of Telamon, king of Salamis. After **Achilles**, he was the bravest of the Greeks. Totally different from the Lesser Ajax, he was noted for his courtesy, piety and good character. Several times he fought against **Hector**, but the gods had decreed that Hector would only fall to Achilles, and so each time he began to be bested they rescued him. Ajax was noted for having taken numerous towns on the coast of Asia Minor.

At the fall of Troy, Ajax suffered a series of setbacks. He demanded that **Helen** be put to death for her adultery, but the brothers **Agamemnon** and **Menelaus** were incensed by this, and **Odysseus** secured her return to Menelaus. Next Ajax demanded the Palladium as his share of the spoils. This was the statue of Pallas upon which Troy's preservation depended and which Odysseus and **Diomedes** had stolen. Once again he was thwarted by Agamemnon and Menelaus, who had to surround themselves with armed guards for protection against him. Another account tells how Ajax coveted the arms of Achilles which, after his death, were to go to the Greek who had most frightened the Trojans. A poll was conducted amongst the Trojan prisoners and they, out of pique, named Odysseus, who duly received the armor. That night Ajax, in a fit of madness, killed the entire flock of sheep intended to feed the Greeks, imagining it to be his enemies. In the morning, realizing the lengths to which he had been driven, he fell on his sword and committed suicide.

ALCMAEON

Like many of the Greek heroes, Alcmaeon found himself in difficulties through no fault of his own. His father was the prophet Amphiarus, who knew that if he participated in the war of the Seven Against Thebes he would die. He therefore concealed himself, but his whereabouts were betrayed by his wife, Eriphyle, who was seduced by the gift of a magnificent gold necklace by Polynices. Amphiarus went to war, but told Alcmaeon that when he heard the news of his father's death he should kill his mother in vengeance. This he duly did and was consequently pursued by the **Furies** because of his matricide. He was to receive purification from the river god Phlegeus, whose daughter Alphesiboea he married and to whom he gave his mother's necklace. His land, however, was struck with barrenness and another oracle said that he had to be purified again, but this time by the river god Achelous. After much wandering he found the god, who purified him and gave him his daughter Callirrhoe in marriage. She demanded as a gift the famous necklace. Alcmaeon, in a quandary, retrieved the object from Alphesiboea, upon the pretext of having to dedicate it to **Apollo** at Delphi in final atonement. Phlegeus agreed to this, but subsequently found out the truth of the matter. He therefore had his sons murder Alcmaeon, whose body was left unburied and prey to wild animals. Alcmaeon's sons by Callirrhoe then avenged their father's murder by killing the murderers.

AMMUT

Egyptian goddess of the Underworld. Upon the physical death of a person a number of entities still continued to live. One element, known as the Ateh, descended into the Underworld where it negotiated dangerous paths, lakes of fire, and doorways guarded by ferocious armed deities, and eventually came into the Hall of Two Truths. There a tribunal of 42 assessor gods examined the dead man's earthly life to judge if he deserved to spend eternity in the realm of **Osiris**. This entitled the heart, considered to be the record of all past deeds, to be weighed in a pair of scales against the goddess of Truth. Provided the dead man's statements were truthful the scales balanced and the god Thoth declared him "True of voice" and fit for the kingdom of Osiris. Ammut sat by the scales during the proceedings. She had the head of a crocodile, the body of a lion or leopard, and the rear-end of a hippopotamus, and devoured those hearts that failed the examination, which caused all other parts of the soul to perish. Her name is usually translated as "Devouress of the Dead" or "She who Gobbles Down."

AMUN

An Egyptian deity who combined with the sun god to become Amun-Re, Amun

Head of Amun.

Amun, Mut and Khonsu.

was paramount in the Egyptian pantheon during the height of the pharaonic empire. He was an anthropomorphic god, sporting a crown of two tall plumes. His name means "The Hidden One," and gives little clue to his vital personality. He was also a war god, instigating attack and an impregnable bulwark for the defense of the royal warrior, being particularly associated with the military operations of Tutmose III, when Egyptian dominion stretched from the Sudan to Syria, and with the less successful campaigns of Rameses II against the Hittites. Scenes on the walls of Deir-el Bahari and Luxor stress this close relationship. The most magnificent of the many temples dedicated to Amun was that of Karnak at Eastern Thebes. Every year the New Year festival procession left the precinct of Karnak to travel by road and river to Luxor, with Amun's cult statue being towed on a magnificent 100-foot gilded barge.

ANDROMEDA

In Greek myth the daughter of Cepheus, king of Ethiopia, and Cassiopia. She claimed to be more beautiful than all the Nereids put together, so they called upon **Poseidon** to avenge this slur upon them. He sent a sea monster to ravage the land and the oracle of Ammon, when approached, said that the beast could only be appeased by offering Andromeda to it. She was consequently chained to a rock to await the monster. At the time **Perseus**, mounted on the flying horse **Pegasus**, was returning from dealing with the **Gorgon** and saw the girl. He fell in love with her and offered her father to free her if she married him. This was agreed and he straightway displayed the Gorgon's head to the monster, who was turned to stone. The couple returned to Argos and subsequently to Tiryns and had several sons. Other versions of the legend locate Cepheus' kingdom in Phoenicia, on the

A

Andromeda being rescued by Theseus.

Palestinian coast, and Andromeda's rock at Joppa.

ANTIGONE

Daughter of the Greek king **Oedipus** by his incestuous union with his mother Jocasta, Antigone was the epitome of the dutiful daughter and sister. When her father realized his great crime and blinded himself in remorse, she traveled with him around the countryside until his death. Returning to Thebes in Boetia, she lived with her sister, Ismene, and found, in the war of the Seven Against Thebes, that her two brothers Eteocles and Polynices, were on opposing sides. They met in combat before the gates of the city.

ANUBIS

Egyptian jackal god responsible for the processes of embalming and the protection of the desert necropolis. The black coat of Anubis contrasts with the natural tawny color of jackals to indicate the idea of resurrection in the next life in an analogy to the life-supporting fertility of the black Nile silt. It also hinted at the darkening hue of the corpses after mummification. His association with the funerary cult may have originated with the depredation of jackals, hyenas, and desert dogs in pre-dynastic burial grounds. As "The One in Front of the Gods' Pavilion," Anubis presided over the embalming tents, while as "Lord of the Sacred Land," his jurisdiction over the tombs was acknowledged. He dispensed the necessary fragrant oils for the embalmers to rub into the corpses and was also responsible for the wrapping of the body in linen bandages woven by the goddess Tayet. Beyond the tomb, Anubis guided the deceased in the Underworld toward the throne of **Osiris** once the Weighing of the Heart ceremony had been successfully negotiated.

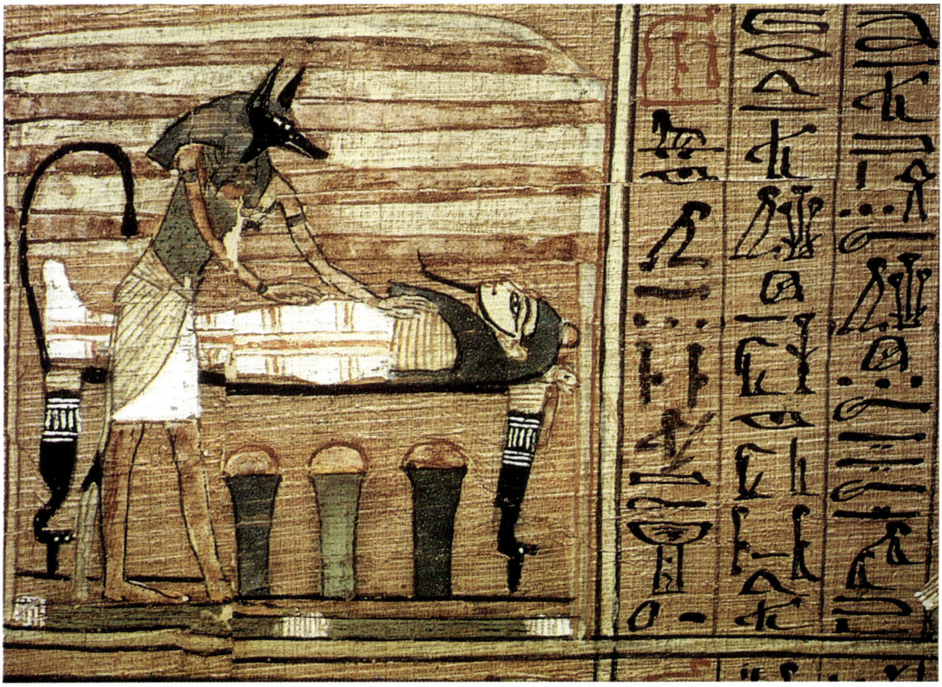

Jackal-headed Anubis, the god of embalming.

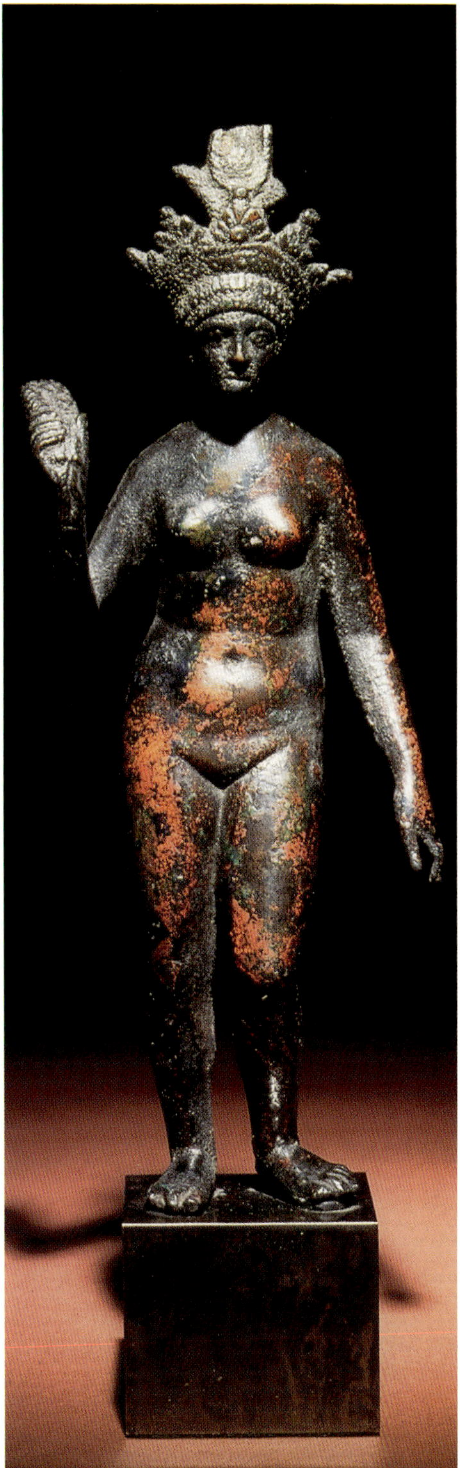

Aphrodite.

ANZU (or ZU)

Also Imdugud, the Thunderbird of Sumerian mythology, a gigantic lion-headed bird-like figure who was conceived as a manifestation of the gods Ningirsu and later **Ninurta**. A famous relief discovered in a Sumerian temple at Ubaid in southern Iraq, which dates to the early third millennium BC, gives a good idea of his appearance, This mythological figure was responsible for stealing the Tablet of Destinies from **Enlil**, later recovered by Ninurta, in a myth attested in both Sumerian and Akkadian versions.

APHRODITE

Greek goddess of love and beauty, the daughter of **Zeus** by Dione. The best known account of her birth has her rising from the sea foam at Paphos on the coast of Cyprus. She was married to the smith god **Hephaestus**, but left him for the war-god **Ares**, by whom she had five children, **Eros** being the best known. Among her other lovers were **Adonis** and Anchises, by whom she had **Aeneas**.

Her favors lay with the Trojans during the Trojan War and especially with Aeneas. Her award of the Apple of Discord in the judgment of **Paris** between the goddesses **Hera**, **Aphrodite**, and **Athena** led to the abduction of **Helen**, and was the cause of the Trojan War. She was particularly prone to angry outbursts and gods as well as mortals suffered because of it.

APIS

In Egyptian mythology the creator-god **Ptah** of Memphis had as his herald the bull-god Apis to communicate with mankind on his behalf in the delivery of oracles. Memphis was the administrative and political capital of the country,

Aphrodite, goddess of love..

Apis, bull god of Memphis.

so the cult of the Apis bull became the most prestigious animal cult in the land. The birth of the Apis bull was a miraculous event: its mother, the Isis cow as she came to be called, conceived her calf through being struck by lightning. Traditionally the Apis bull bore particular markings consisting of a completely black hide except for a white triangle on its forehead, and the tip of its tail dividing into two thick strands. Its divinity was enhanced by a garment on its back in the design of the wings of a vulture goddess.

APOLLO

Greek god, the son of **Leto** by **Zeus**, had **Artemis** as his slightly older twin sister. They were born on the island of Delos, under the shade of the only tree that grew on it, a palm. Apollo's major shrine was at Delphi, but before this could be established he had first to vanquish a monster, the dragon/serpent called Python, which terrorized the local countryside. He slew the creature, but to pacify its spirit inaugurated the Pythgian Games at Delphi in its honor. Delphi became noted throughout the Ancient World for the oracular pronouncements made by the priestess, the Pythia, in a hallucinatory state. All levels of society sent there for advice, which was usually of an ambiguous nature, for the supplicant to interpret as best he could. In the legends **Heracles** once came to consult the oracle and dissatisfied with his answer, attempted to steal the sacred tripod, emblem of Apollo. The god and the hero fought over the tripod (a scene often depicted in ancient art on coins and pottery), but Zeus separated them and the tripod remained at Delphi.

Apollo was also the god of music, fine arts, poetry, and eloquence. Like his sister, Artemis, he was a hunter, and together they slew with their arrows the children of **Niobe**, after she had insulted their mother Leto. As the god of music he presided over the nine Muses on Mount Parnassus. He was also the god of medicine, who could cure as well as kill. Responsibility for the plague that struck the Greeks at Troy (Apollo favored the Trojans) lay with him, and he used it to force them to return the daughter of his priest Chryses. He had a number of encounters with mankind, working at times for kings as a herdsman, and several love affairs with mortal girls and nymphs, a number of whom assumed other shapes in an endeavor to escape his attentions.

In later legend he was closely associated with **Orpheus** and thereby with an eternal life concept.

APOPHIS

In Egyptian mythology a gigantic serpent whose nature symbolized the idea of chaos and non-existence, whom all Egyptians dreaded. When **Re** the sun god descended behind Bakhu, the mountain of the west, to travel the 12 hours of night through the Underworld, Apophis lay in wait in order to swallow him. The sun god was towed along on a boat, but his crew became hypnotized by the stare of Apophis. The rescuer of Re was the god **Set**, whose strength and pugnacity matched that of Apophis. Set subdued the serpent by intoning a magical chant while sticking a spear down its throat.

ARES

Greek god of war, the son of **Zeus** and his wife **Hera**. His brother was **Hephaestus**, the smith god. Always represented armed, he was prone to launch himself into a cause by inquiring too closely as to its validity. He was often at loggerheads with his half-sister, **Athena**, and in the Trojan War they supported different sides, he favoring the Trojans. He had a daughter, Harmonia, as a result of an affair with **Aphrodite**, who married **Cadmus**, king of Thrace, an area particularly associated with Ares. Most of his children by mortal women were of a violent nature.

The hill in Athens where religious crimes were tried in antiquity, the Areopagus, takes its name from the fact that Ares was tried there for the murder of Halirrhotius and acquitted by the Olympian gods on a verdict of what today would be called "justifiable homicide."

ARGONAUTS

The name given to the crew of the ship *Argo* who accompanied **Jason** to Colchis on his quest for the Golden Fleece. The *Argo* was a 40-oared ship built at Pagasae in Thessaly by Argos. **Athena** supervised the construction and herself brought a piece of oak from **Zeus**' sacred tree, the Oak of Dodona. She gave the wood the power of speech and then had it carved into the prow. This was to prove extremely useful on the voyage, since it was able to warn Jason and his crew of impending dangers en route.

The crew included several well-known names such as **Heracles** and the **Dioscuri**. Jason is generally the prime mover and focus of most of their adventures, especially in his association with **Medea** and **Circe**.

Apollo, lord of light, music and phrophecy.

Artemis, sistyer of Apollo.

The voyage of the Argonauts went up the Black Sea to Colchis, where the quest was fulfilled, and then followed a circuitous route home that included southern Italy, North Africa, and Crete. The whole episode lasted about four months. After they arrived back at Iolchos with the Golden Fleece, Jason sailed the *Argo* to Corinth, where it was dedicated to **Poseidon**. The story is a navigational epic that has parallels in other mythologies, particularly Celtic. Its origins are earlier than the *Odyssey*, which refers to it, and gives a great deal of important background to the Greek world at the time.

ARIADNE

Daughter of King **Minos** of Crete and **Pasiphae**. In the legend of **Theseus** she fell in love with him when he came with the other tribute youths and maidens from Athens to Crete to be sent into the Labyrinth to the Minotaur. Theseus promised to marry her if she helped him. She gave him a ball of thread and a sword, the former to be paid out as he entered the Labyrinth to help him find his way out after he had slain the Minotaur. Theseus succeeded and left Crete with Ariadne. However, he abandoned her on the island of Naxos, leaving her sleeping on the shore. **Dionysus**, the god of wine, passing by was captivated by her beauty, woke her and married her. They are often represented together on Greek wine-drinking vessels.

ARTEMIS

Daughter of the Greek god **Zeus** and **Leto**, and slightly older twin sister of **Apollo**, born on the island of Delos (out of the way of a jealous and wrathful Hera). She was the eternal virgin huntress-goddess, but she had a somewhat vindictive nature; the deaths of **Actaeon**, Callisto, **Meleager**, the children of Niobe, and Orion were due to her. In revenge for **Agamemnon**'s boast at Aulis that he had killed a fine stag (the animal that is associated with Artemis), she becalmed the Greek fleet on the way to Troy until **Iphigenia** had been brought to her.

At Ephesus, Artemis was worshipped more as the Asiatic mother-goddess than the Greek huntress-goddess, although stags were still associated with her, as were bees. Her temple there was listed as one of the Seven Wonders of the Ancient World and her cult statue, of which numerous later copies exist, was a curious statue noted for its many breasts and polos headdress.

ASCELPIUS

Or Aesculapius, son of Coronis—whose father, Phlelegyas, was king of Thessaly—and the Greek god **Apollo**. The god seduced the girl, but then became angry when he found she had a mortal lover. He caused her death by lightning but saved the child, whom he gave to the Centaur **Chiron** to educate in the art of medicine. He was an exceptional pupil and was even able to bring the dead back to life, by using blood from the right-side veins of the **Gorgon** given him by **Athena**. **Pluto**, god of the dead, complained to his brother **Zeus**, who was not prepared to allow this situation to continue and he therefore struck Ascelpius with a thunderbolt. Apollo was incensed at the death of his son, but could do nothing against Zeus, so instead he killed the Cyclops who had made the thunderbolt.

After his death, Ascelpius received divine honors and was changed into a constellation. His most famous shrine was at Epidaurus where there are still

Ascelpius, god of medecine and healing.

extensive remains today. A number of gods from other religions were assimilated with him in the classical period, the Egyptian god **Imhotep** for example.

ATALANTA

Greek princess with various parents, according to the legends, but probably the best claim is that of Schoenus, king of Boetia. Her father wanted only boys, so she was abandoned at birth and fed by a she-bear until she was found by hunters, who brought her up. Wishing to remain a virgin, she dedicated herself to the huntress-goddess **Artemis**. She was present at the great Calydonian Boar hunt with the other heroes and is said to have been the first to wound it. Its head was given to her as a present by Meleager, who actually killed it and was himself to perish shortly afterward.

Such was her beauty that Atalanta had many suitors, but she rejected them all on the grounds of her vow—or because she had been told that if she married she would be turned into an animal. To dissuade suitors she agreed to marry only he who could outrun her; any who failed, as many did despite the fact that she gave them a head-start, forfeited their lives. A fresh suitor, Melanion (sometimes given as Hippomanes), however, had her measure. **Aphrodite** had given him three golden apples from the garden of the Hesperides. These he took to the contest with him and as soon as he felt Atalanta gaining on him in the race, he dropped the apples one by one. She stopped to pick them up—either from avarice or because she wished to let him win. He thus won the race and her hand in marriage. Some time later, while out hunting together, the pair entered a sanctuary of **Zeus** (some legends say **Cybele**) and there made love. Affronted at such sacrilege, Zeus changed them both into lions, so fulfilling Atalanta's fear concerning marriage.

ATEN

Briefly the ascendant deity in Egyptian mythology, his name means the "Disk of the Sun." His cult saw worship of a creator god close to (but not quite reaching) monotheism. The iconography of the god Aten took the form of the solar disk with rays emanating from it which ended in hands. Those hands approaching figures of royalty were depicted as holding out the ankh—the sign of eternal life. It was during the reign of Tutmose IV that Aten begins his rise toward ascendant deity and the god's progress continued during the subsequent reign of Amenhotep III, who changed his name to Akhenaten. The god's cult died with this strange ruler and orthodox polytheism returned.

ATHENA

Greek goddess of wisdom, the daughter of Metis by **Zeus**, she had a strange birth. Zeus had been warned that should Metis give birth to a daughter, she would be followed by a son who would oust his father. To thwart the prophecy, Zeus swallowed the infant just as Metis was about to give birth. He then developed a headache, so **Hephaestus** took a double-headed ax and split his skull open and out leapt the goddess Athena, fully grown and armed.

Athens, Athena's premier city and sanctuary, with the Parthenon built on its Acropolis, was won by the goddess in a contest with **Poseidon**. They contested the sovereignty of Attica and it was decided that whoever produced the better gift for mankind would be declared the winner. Poseidon struck a rock with his trident and a horse sprang forth

Athena, patroness of the city of Athens.

Helmeted Athena.

(some versions say it was a salt-water spring on the Acropolis); Athena caused an olive tree to grow there. The gods judged the olive was the best gift and Athena won the city.

As a warlike goddess she was the protector of many towns and heroes. In the Trojan War she sided with the Greeks because she could not forgive **Paris** for not awarding her the golden apple. She especially watched over **Achilles** and **Odysseus**, helping them both during the war and Odysseus also during his 10-year journey home to Ithaca afterward. Although she supported the Greeks, it was an ancient form of her image as Pallas, referred to as the Palladium, that kept Troy safe while it remained in the city. Hence the reason why Odysseus and **Diomedes** stole it one night.

Her familiar bird was the owl, which, along with her head, became the city badge of the coins of Athens. Her breastplate was the aegis made of goatskin and on the front of her shield she carried the head of the Gorgon **Medusa**, which **Perseus** had given her.

ATLAS

A giant in Greek myth, the son of the sea nymph Clymene and Iapetus. By his wife Pleione, daughter of Oceanus, he had seven children. He fought against the gods in the great battle between gods and giants, and as punishment **Zeus** condemned him to carry the sky on his shoulders. He is also said to have been a king in North Africa who refused hospitality to **Perseus** upon his return from slaying the Gorgon **Medusa**. Perseus therefore showed him Medusa's head and turned him to stone, thus creating the Atlas mountains that stretch across North Africa.

ATRA-HASIS

Exceedingly wise hero of the Akkadian myth first attested in cuneiform tablets of the 17th century BC, which began "When the gods like man." The story, still partly unrecovered, tells of the period in the mists of time before the appearance of man, when the gods had to fend for themselves. The junior gods responsible for the harder work rebelled and so the chief gods decided to create mankind to do the work for them. Enki and the principal mother-goddess made a man out of clay like a figurine, animated with flesh and blood taken from an obscure god called We-ila, with their divine saliva. Having produced the human prototype, a group of mother-goddesses worked to make seven males and seven females. A brick structure mentioned in this connection evidently corresponds to the brick birth couch used in Mesopotamian society.

The human race, once set on its path, multiplied rapidly, to the point where the hubbub disturbed the gods, who were prompted to return to desperate remedies. Plague, drought, and famine were unsuccessfully tried by **Enlil** to dispose of the human nuisance, but each time he was foiled by Enki, who was determined to protect the human race through the king, Atra-Hasis. Finally Enlil resolved to destroy mankind with a flood. The description of the flood in this myth is closely related to, and indeed provided the source for, that in the *Epic of* ***Gilgamesh***. Atra-Hasis, guided by Enki, built a boat from the reeds of his house, and sealed it with pitch. He then took on board his family, goods and chattels, and healthy examples of animals and birds, before the flood arrived destroying all life on Earth. Rain fell for seven days and seven nights, and the interruption of their regular offerings made some of the gods regret their hasty decision to dispense with their human servants. The description of the settling of the boat and decline of the waters in the Gilgamesh version is still missing from the sources of this myth. Once landed Atra-Hasis craftily sacrificed at once to the hungry gods, who were attracted "like flies" to the smell of the food.

ATREUS

In Greek myth, the father of **Agamemnon** and **Menelaus** (the Atridae). He had been the king of Pisa, but having been involved in the murder of his half-brother Chrysippus, he had fled to Mycenae where he married Aerope, daughter of King Eurystheor, whom he succeeded on the throne. The family history then becomes horrendous and complicated. Atreus' brother, Thyestes, followed him to Mycenae and had an affair with his wife, Aerope. Having found out about it, Atreus pretended to forgive his brother and invited him to a banquet. He served a dish of stewed meat and after Thyestes had eaten it Atreus displayed to him the heads of his three sons, whom he had just eaten. Thyestes fled to the court of Sicyon, where, without knowing her identity, he fathered a son, Aegisthus, on his own daughter, Pelopea. Shortly afterward she married Atreus, whose first wife, Aerope, had died. Atreus adopted Aegisthus without knowing who his father was and sent him to murder Thyestes. Thyestes knew that Aegisthus was his own son and revealed himself; Aegisthus therefore changed tack and returned to Mycenae and murdered Atreus. A large tholos tomb at Mycenae is called the "Treasury of Atreus" although it has no known connection with him.

ATROPOS

One of the Three Fates (the Moirai to the Greeks; to the Romans they were the Parcae), along with her sisters Clotho and Lachsis. They were the daughters of **Zeus** and Themis, goddess of Law. Atropos was the eldest sister, who snipped through the thread of each man's life with a pair of scissors.

ATUM

In Egyptian mythology one form that the sun god **Re** was thought to take was that of Atum "Lord of Heliopolis," a primeval creator-god. Self-engendered he rose up out of the primeval waters, an analogy of the Nile inundation, and masturbated. The falling semen transmuted into the air god **Shu** and the moisture goddess **Tefnut**, who in turn produced the earth god **Geb** and the sky goddess **Nut**.

B

BAAL

This name, the general Semitic word for "lord" or "master," is applied especially to Baal-Hadad, the Canaanite storm and weather god, and indeed king of the gods, well known from the mythological texts of the second millennium BC from Ugarit (Ras Shamra). Of probable West-Semitic or Amorite origin, he is described in Ugaritic texts as "the most powerful of heroes" and "the one who rides the clouds." He was the son of Dagon, and brother to the "virgin" Anath, and the hero of a great complicated mythological epic, written over seven cuneiform tablets.

A great temple was built for him, but Baal was slain by monsters and carried off to the Land of Death. As a result, all life on earth was grievously affected, so Anath found Mot, the god of Death, and slaughtered him after a fierce battle. Mot's body was cut up, winnowed, burned, ground up and sowed in the ground and by this means, Baal was revived.

The cat goddess Bastet.

BACCHUS

Son of **Jupiter** and **Semele** and the Roman equivalent of the Greek god of wine, **Dionysus**. He shared the same attributes and most of the legends of his precursor. In the Roman world, and especially in Roman North Africa, he was often known as Liber Pater, after an old Italian god. The Bacchanalia, an orgiastic and drunken celebration of the god, reached such heights that it had to be banned by the Roman Senate in 186 BC.

BASTET

Originally in Egyptian mythology a lioness, who modified into the more benign cat-goddess in the first millennium BC. In her early occurrences Bastet, daughter of **Re**, the sun-god, was a royal protectress, her name is carved on the northern facade of the granite valley temple of King Khafre at Giza, counterbalancing the southern goddess **Hathor**. In the north-east Delta there stood an impressive temple with ceremonial halls of granite, which was sacred to Bastet. This temple at Bubastis once witnessed

Bacchus the god of wine and song.

riotous festivals of music and dancing described in the fifth century BC by the Greek historian Herodotus. Sacred cats kept near the temples were buried in cemeteries and cats were revered in the household. Mummified cats were frequently elaborately wrapped with the linen bandages forming geometric patterns. The Ancient Egyptian sense of humor comes across in the faces painted on these cat mummies, which express bewilderment, indignation, or an enchanting smile.

BELLEROPHON

Greek hero and son of Glaucus, king of Corinth, and Eurymede. In his youth Bellerophon accidentally killed a man and had to leave Corinth. He made his way to Tiryns (an old Mycenaean citadel in Argos) and the court of King Proteus, who purified him of the murder. Unfortunately, the king's wife, Anteia, made advances toward Bellerophon, and when he rejected her, she accused him of trying to seduce her. Her husband could not avenge the charge as Bellerophon was his guest, so he sent him to his father-in-law Iobates, king of Lycia and Anteia's father, with a letter asking that the bearer be killed. Iobates, reading it and believing the charge made against Bellerophon, sent him to kill the Chimaera. This was a monstrous beast, part lion, part dragon, with a flame-throwing goat's head sprouting from the middle of its back, which was laying waste the countryside. Bellerophon found the winged horse **Pegasus** drinking at the Pirene spring in Corinth and captured it. He was thus able to successfully attack the Chimaera, avoiding its dangerous goat's head, and kill it.

In a second attempt to have Bellerophon killed, Iobates sent him against his warlike neighbors the Solymi. This also failed, as did the next one against the Amazons. Finally an ambush was laid by the best of the Lydian warriors, but they also fell to Bellerophon. The king realized that the

Bellerophon slaying the Chimaera.

gods were protecting the innocent and he gave Bellerophon his daughter Philonoe in marriage and made him heir to the kingdom of Lycia. A late aspect of the legend says that Bellerophon, in old age, tried to ride his winged horse into the lands of the gods. For his presumption Zeus hurled him back into the sea, where he drowned.

BELLONA

The Roman goddess of war, often depicted as the wife of **Mars**, sometimes as his sister. Her Greek equivalent was Enyo, often represented covered in blood. Bellona was sometimes shown on the reverse of Roman Republic silver coins.

BES

Egyptian deity particularly relevant to the ordinary Egyptians since he was responsible for the prosperity of the family and in particular the welfare of children. He is unmistakable in his iconography: a huge-bellied dwarf with bandy legs, whose face is a hybrid of human and leonine characteristics. He can bare his fangs, protrude his tongue and brandish a dagger, but all this aggression is directed to thwart evil forces that might endanger the family. His image decorated the walls of bedrooms, as indicated in the excavations of the village of the workmen at Deir el-Bahari in Western Thebes. He also appeared on utilitarian objects, such as headrests, mirrors, cosmetic spoons, and tubes for eye-paint and makeup. In Ptolemaic and Roman cult temples, such as the temple of **Hathor** at Dendera, an important element was the sanctuary celebrating the birth of the child of the principal god and goddess. Over the entrance the effigy of Bes was cut to ward off any hostile being from harming the divine child whose birth was celebrated inside.

Egyptian dwarf god Bes.

C

CADMUS

A Greek hero whose sister **Europa** was abducted by **Zeus** in the shape of a bull. He was the son of Agenor, king of Phoenicia, and Telephassa. Cadmus' father sent him and his brothers in search of their sister, ordering them not to return without her. The quest was impossible and the oracle suggested that Cadmus should found a city by following a cow until it stopped from exhaustion. He found a cow wandering off by itself which had the mark of the moon in white on each of its flanks. This he took to be an omen and followed it as directed. When the site for the city had been identified, Cadmus sent some of his companions to seek water to be used in an offering to the gods. Since they were a long time returning, he went in search of them and found

Telemachus encountering Calypso.

they had been attacked by a dragon that guarded the pool. He slew it with **Athena**'s assistance, who then said that he should sew the dragon's teeth. Immediately there sprang up a number of armed warriors who began advancing on Cadmus. Quick-wittedly he threw a large stone into their midst and they started fighting among themselves. The five that survived became his companions, one of them, Echion, ultimately marrying one of Cadmus' daughters, Agave.

Cadmus set about building the city, which became Thebes in Boetia. Zeus gave him Harmonia—the daughter of **Aphrodite** by **Ares**—for his wife, and he had a son, Polydorus, and four daughters. One of them, **Semele**, was to become the mother of **Dionysus** by Zeus. In old age Cadmus and Harmonia left Thebes, some accounts say because of **Hera**'s persecution of their children, and went to live in Illyrium. A prophecy had said that they should live where the Illyrians would be victorious over their rivals, the Encheleans. This came about and Cadmus ruled in Illyria, producing another Illyrius. Subsequently, Cadmus and his wife were changed into serpents that were sent to the Elysian fields (the heaven of Ancient Greece).

CALYPSO

A Greek nymph, the daughter of **Atlas** and Pleione, who lived on the island of Ogygia in the western Mediterranean (actually the peninsula of Ceuta opposite Gibraltar). **Odysseus**, in his wanderings after the fall of Troy, arrived there and Calypso fell in love with him. By her enchantment she was able to keep him with her for seven (perhaps ten) years. Eventually, on the plea of **Athena**, who always looked after Odysseus' interests, **Hermes** was sent by **Zeus** to persuade Calypso to let him depart, which she did, providing Odysseus with wood for a raft and food for his journey.

CASSANDRA

Daughter of **Priam**, king of Troy, and Hecuba, and beloved of **Apollo**. She resisted his advances and he offered her the gift of prophecy if she would yield to him; however, having received the gift, she changed her mind and continued to refuse him. He could not withdraw the gift, but he could change it; although she would prophesy accurately, Apollo decreed that no one would believe her. She foretold that **Paris** would bring about the downfall of Troy and that **Helen**'s abduction would be the cause. When the Greeks made the Wooden Horse in an attempt to trick their way into the city, Cassandra and the priest Laocoon cried out against bringing it into the city. **Hera** sent snakes to destroy Laocoon and his family and no one believed Cassandra when she said the horse was full of armed warriors.

At the fall of Troy, Cassandra took refuge at the statue of **Athena**, where she was found by the Lesser **Ajax**, who committed sacrilege when he raped her. Cassandra became the property of **Agamemnon** when the spoils were divided and he took her back with him to Mycenae. She had also prophesied that his wife, **Clytemnestra**, would kill him, which she duly did, together with Cassandra.

CERBERUS

The three-headed monster who in Greek myth guarded the entrance to **Hades** had curious parents. His father was the multi-headed giant Typhon and his mother was Echidna, a beautiful woman above the waist, but a serpent below. Cerberus' task was to prevent the living

Three headed Cerebus, guardian of Hell's portal.

entering the kingdom of Hades and to make sure that none of the dead escaped from it. It was one of the labors of **Heracles** to bring Cerberus up from the Underworld to King Eurytheus, which he did with Hades' permission so long as he did not use any weapons to subdue the beast. Heracles half-throttled all three heads and dragged him up before Eurytheus, who promptly dived into a large jar in terror: a very popular scene in Greek vase painting. **Orpheus** charmed Cerberus with the music of his lyre, and so was able to enter the Underworld in search of Eurydice.

Ceres, mother of Penelope.

CERES

The Roman equivalent of the Greek **Demeter**, the goddess of corn and the harvest. She shares the same legends and sanctuaries as her Greek counterpart.

CHARON

The ferryman in Greek legend who took the souls of the dead across the marshes of Acheron and the River Styx to the Underworld. His parents were brother and sister, Erebus and Nox, the children of Chaos. He was represented as a disreputable, filthy old man with a straggly beard and tattered clothes who bullied the souls, his passengers; they not only had to pay his fee for the crossing but also row themselves. The fee, a small silver coin called an obol, was often put under the tongue of the corpse. When **Heracles** went down into the Underworld to retrieve **Cerberus**, Charon refused him passage across the Styx but Heracles beat him so violently with his own ferryhook that he had to succumb. For allowing a living being into Hades, Charon was sentenced to be chained for a year.

Charon, with Hermes on the left.

Circe offers magic potion to Odysseus.

CHIRON
A Centaur, half man and half horse, the son of **Cronus** and Philyra. His curious form came about because his father had coupled with his mother in the shape of a horse. Chiron was born immortal, but was always interested in and kindly toward humans. He was famous for his wisdom and his knowledge of music, medicine, and ethics. Many of the great heroes of mythology were his pupils. These included **Achilles**, **Aeneas**, **Ascelpius**, **Heracles**, **Jason**, and **Peleus**. Chiron was credited with the introducion of surgery when he replaced a damaged bone in Achilles' ankle with a section from that of a giant.

Not all the Centaurs were as amiable as Chiron. Some were rapacious and unruly, as the classic battle between the Lapiths and Centaurs shows (carved on reliefs from the Parthenon and the temple of **Apollo** at Bassae, Greece). At the Massacre of the Centaurs they were pursued by Heracles with his magic bow. Unfortunately Chiron, standing by Heracles, was accidentally wounded in the knee by an arrow. Even his medical skills with ointments could not heal a wound from Heracles' arrow. The pain was excruciating and Chiron retreated to a cave, imploring **Zeus** to take away his immortality so that he could die. His wish was granted and he was placed among the constellations as Sagittarius, the Archer.

CIRCE
Greek princess noted for her command of the magic arts. She was the daughter of the Sun and Perseis, and the sister of Aetes, king of Colchis (who kept the Golden Fleece retrieved by **Jason**) and **Pasiphae**, the wife of **Minos**, king of Crete. She lived on the island of Aeaea. **Odysseus** landed near her palace and sent some men to reconnoiter. One, Eurylochus, more cautious than the rest, stayed back as the group was invited into palace. They were feasted with

meat and wine and then Circe touched each of them with her wand, changing them into various animals reflecting their individual natures. Eurylochus fled back to Odysseus and told him what he had seen.

Resolving to save his companions, Odysseus was making his way through the woods when he met the god **Mercury**, who told him how to break Circe's spells. Odysseus was given a herb to put secretly into the wine Circe would give him. This would make him impervious to her spells and he was then to draw his sword and threaten her life. All worked as Mercury had said. Circe's spell was broken and, under threat from Odysseus' sword, she vowed not to harm any of the men and to change them back into their human form. They then stayed a while with her, the outcome of which was that Circe had two children by Odysseus, a son named Telegonus (who became a founder of Tusculum) and a daughter, Cassiphone.

Circe was also involved with Jason and the **Argonauts** upon their return journey from Colchis. They landed there because Circe was **Medea**'s aunt.

CLOTHO

The youngest of the three Fates, the Greek Moirai, Roman Parcae. Her sisters were **Atropos** and **Lachesis**. They were the children of **Zeus** and Themis, goddess of law. Clotho was always represented with a distaff because it was she that spun the thread of a man's life.

CLYTEMNESTRA

A major figure in the story of the Trojan War. She was the daughter of Tyndareus, king of Sparta, and **Leda**. **Helen** was her half-sister and the **Dioscuri** her half-brothers by **Zeus** and Leda. Her first husband was **Tantalus**, but he and their children were killed by **Agamemnon**, who then married her. When Agamemnon left for Troy with his brother **Menelaus**, he left Clytemnestra

Orestes kills Clytemnestra.

in the care of his cousin Aegisthus, who formed a liaison with her. Upon Agamemnon's return to Argos after the fall of Troy she plotted with Aegisthus to murder him. Together they killed him with axes while he struggled to put on a shirt she had sewn up to confuse him. **Cassandra**, who had been brought from Troy as spoils-of-war, was also murdered by the pair.

Clytemnestra's hatred then turned toward her children by Agamemnon. Her daughter, **Electra**, was imprisoned at Mycenae, but the boy, **Orestes**, escaped and later in life returned, seeking vengeance for his father's murder. He killed his mother and her lover, and the **Furies** then pursued him for his crime of matricide.

Cupid, Roman god of love.

CRONUS

Saturn to the Romans, was the youngest of the six Titans born to **Uranus** and **Gaia**. Incited by his mother, he castrated his father and took his place as king, but continued in the same despotic way until Gaia plotted a second revolution. Cronus married his sister Rhea and began to produce children. However, Uranus and Gaia told him that he would be overthrown by one of his own children, so he took to swallowing them as they were born. Five were dispatched this way (Hestia, **Demeter**, **Hera**, **Hades**, and **Poseidon**). With the coming of the sixth child, Rhea fled to Crete in an endeavor to protect it. The child, **Zeus**, was born on Crete in the Dikte Cave; to deceive Cronus who came looking for him, Rhea gave him a stone heavily wrapped in cloths, which he swallowed. Zeus grew in secrecy and then gave Cronus a potion that made him regurgitate the other five children. They all then declared war on Cronus and with the aid of those children of Gaia that Cronus had imprisoned, they defeated and killed him. Thus the second major line of Greek gods reigned, with Zeus at their head. Cronus was also father of the Centaur **Chiron** by Philyra.

CUPID

The Roman god of love, equivalent to the Greek **Eros**, whose mother was **Venus** (**Aphrodite**) and his father variously given in the legends as **Jupiter** (**Zeus**), **Mars** (**Ares**) or **Mercury** (**Hermes**). He is usually represented as a small, chubby naked child, armed with a bow and arrows. Mischievously, he would aim "Cupid's darts" at will, at times causing untold mayhem as they caused those pierced to fall in love with the first person they met. In classical art he is often shown playing a game such as quoits, but sometimes he wears a helmet and carries a spear and shield to show that even Mars, god of war, gives way to love. His encounter with **Psyche** shows him in a more serious aspect.

CYBELE

Syrian mother or earth goddess, variously described as the mother and the lover of the resurrected god Atis. In one legend Atis was so harassed by the attentions of a loving monster that he castrated himself. In another version he was put to death because of his love for Cybele, daughter of the king of Phrygia and Lydia. Cybele equates with **Ishtar**, **Isis**, and Rhea. Her sanctuary was at Pessinus in Phrygia, and her priests were eunuchs. She was attended by lions, and the castration, death, and rebirth of her lover was celebrated annually as part of the seasonal cycle of decay and regeneration. The ceremonies were bloody: rams were sacrificed, and their blood used for baptism, and the initiates used the sickle-shaped knife associated with the goddess for ritual castration. The cult of Cybele was introduced into Rome in 205 BC, and, like those of Isis and **Mithras**, attracted a considerable following.

Cybele in a chariot drawn by lions.

D

DAEDALUS (See ICARUS)
A genius craftsman of the classical world who could turn his hand, and mind, to almost anything. It was said that he was the only one who could create a golden honeycomb in openwork gold, apparently using an actual honeycomb and the lost wax (*cire perdue*) method. He was related to the royal house of Athens, but was exiled for killing his nephew, Talos, in a fit of jealousy because of the talent he showed.

Jupiter and Danae.

Daedalus went to Crete where he found employment with **Minos**, the king. It was Daedalus who constructed the cow in which **Pasiphae**, Minos' queen, could conceal herself, and gratify her passion for her husband's prize bull. The outcome of this liaison was the **Minotaur**, half-bull, and half-man, which Daedalus then had to conceal in the Labyrinth, of which he was the architect. Either for assisting Pasiphae, or for helping **Theseus** by suggesting to **Ariadne** the ball of string trick, Minos imprisoned both Daedalus, and his son **Icarus** (whose mother was a palace slave, Naucrate). They managed to escape by means of large artificial wings, which Daedalus constructed for them both, and which were held together with wax. Daedalus reached Cumae safely, where he built a temple to **Apollo** before flying on to Sicily; but Icarus flew too near the sun, the wax in his wings melted, and he crashed into the sea and drowned.

In Sicily, Daedalus was well received by King Cocalus, but the legends vary about his end. Some say that Cocalus killed him because of his fear of retribution from Minos, others that the daughters of Cocalus killed Minos when he came hunting Daedalus, and that Daedalus expressed his gratitude for their protection by designing many buildings for Cocalus.

DANAE

In Greek myth the daughter of Acrisius, king of Argos, and **Eurydice**. An oracle had told her father that his grandson would kill him. To prevent his daughter conceiving, Acrisius had Danae heavily guarded in an underground room of bronze into which no one was allowed, nor was she allowed out. It was all to no avail; Danae was seduced by **Zeus** in the form of a shower of gold. In fury, when the boy **Perseus** was born, Acrisius had the mother and child cast into the sea in a wooden chest, hoping that the elements would perform the deed that he could not do himself. They were cast upon the shore of the island of Seriphos, and welcomed by Dictys, brother of the local king Polydectes. The latter fell in love with Danae, but feared Perseus, and so sent the boy to seek the head of the **Gorgon**. Upon Perseus' successful return, he and Danae returned to Argos, where he fulfilled the oracle by accidentally killing his grandfather, Acrisius, with a discus.

DAPHNE

A Greek river nymph, one of the many loves of **Apollo**. He pursued the girl, but, just as she was about to be caught, she called out to her father, the River Ladon (sometimes also said to be the River Pheneus), to save her. Either he or the gods heard, and transformed her into a laurel tree. Apollo made a wreath of laurel from its leaves for his head, and decreed that henceforth the tree should be sacred to him.

DEIANIRA

In Greek myth the daughter of Oeneus, king of Calydon, and Althea. She became the wife of **Heracles** after he had gone down into **Hades** in search of **Cerberus**. Her (dead) brother, **Meleager**, met Heracles in Hades, and asked him to marry and look after his sister. This he did, and they had a son, Hyllus. Once, when the couple were traveling together, they came to a swollen mountain stream, and the Centaur Nessus offered to carry Deianira across on his back. Heracles agreed, but when Nessus reached the opposite bank he tried to rape her. Heracles fired one of his magic poisoned arrows at the Centaur, and he fell dying. As he died, he gave his red-dyed tunic to Deianira, telling her that it would win back her husband's love if ever he should be tempted away.

In later years Heracles fell in love with Iole, whom he had won as a prize in an archery competition arranged by her father, Euytus. Deianira therefore sent him the Centaur's tunic as a gift, to win him back, but when Heracles put it on the tunic began to burn his skin, and he could not take it off. In agony, Heracles threw himself onto a funeral pyre on Mount Oeta. Deianira realized that the Centaur had tricked her, and committed suicide in grief.

DEMETER

Sister of the Greek god **Zeus**, and one of the six children of **Cronus** and Rhea, Demeter was the essential mother or fertility goddess, and had many legends associated with her. She has very close parallels with the other major mother-goddess figures of the earlier religions of the Near East, but principally with **Isis** (except that Demeter produced a daughter, **Persephone**, and Isis a son, **Horus**). Persephone's father was Zeus, Demeter's brother, who was married to **Hera**. Mother and daughter are inextricably mixed in the legends. **Hades** (**Pluto**) kidnapped Persephone, taking her down to his underground kingdom

Demeter gives corn to Triptolemus, Persephone at Right.

of the dead to rule there as his consort. Disconsolate, Demeter searched everywhere for her lost daughter, caring nothing for the earth or its crops and harvests. Eventually, Helios, the sun god who sees everything, told her what had happened. Demeter vowed that she would not return to the gods or continue her fertility functions unless her daughter was returned to her. During her absence the earth was barren, and she took work as a wet nurse for Triptolemus—the infant son of Celeus, king of Eleusis, and his wife Metanira. Demeter doted on the child and tried to make him immortal, but his mother intervened (just as happened with Isis and the king of Byblos' son). When at last she discovered her daughter's abductor, Demeter went to Zeus and demanded Persephone's return from the Underworld. Zeus agreed, so long as Persephone had not eaten anything while she was there. All seemed to be well until it was found she had eaten some pips of a pomegranate. Zeus could not therefore keep his promise and Demeter withdrew her support from the Earth. Deadlock had been reached. Demeter did at least instruct the young Triptolemus in agriculture, and gave him corn to take to mankind, but the fields still needed their fertility. Eventually a compromise was reached. Demeter would return to Olympia, and Persephone would be let out from Hades at springtime, when the earth received new vigor, but she had to return later in the year, at harvest-time and when winter approached, reflecting the annual cycle of decay and rebirth.

Demeter's greatest sanctuary was at Eleusis, just outside Athens. Here, the people of Attica came to thank and worship the goddess in the great Eleusian Mysteries. A large cave entrance is still pointed out as one of the entrances to Hades' kingdom of the Underworld.

Demeter seated on a panther.

DEUCALION
The Greek equivalent of the Biblical Noah and Mesopotamian **Utanapishtim**. His father was **Prometheus** and his mother Clymene, daughter of Oceanus. His wife was Pyrrha, the daughter of Epimetheus—a Titan—and **Pandora**. **Zeus** became angry at the vices and irreligious attitudes of mankind, and decided to punish the human race, saving the only two decent people, Deucalion and Pyrrha. He therefore sent a great flood to devastate the earth, but Prometheus had advised Deucalion to build a large chest

Diana, hunting with her hounds.

called an "ark" and save himself and his wife in it. It floated on the waters for nine days and nights, and finally came to rest on the mountains of Thessaly. Zeus then sent his messenger **Hermes** to them and offered to grant them one wish. Deucalion's wish was that they should have some companions. Zeus granted this, but told them the way to effect it was to throw their mother's bones over their shoulders. Pyrrha was horrified at this and could not understand it but Deucalion realized that Zeus meant stones, the "bones" of Mother Earth. This they then did and as they walked along, tossing the stones over their shoulders, men sprang up from those that Deucalion threw and women from those thrown by Pyrrha. Deucalion then became king of Thessaly.

DIANA

The Roman equivalent of the Greek **Artemis**. In the Roman Pantheon her parents were **Jupiter** and Latona whilst in Greek mythology they were **Zeus** and **Leto**. She was the twin sister of **Apollo**, born on the sacred island of Delos. In her Roman aspect, Diana was also the goddess of hunting and she had two particular shrines in Italy: one at Aricia on the shores of Lake Nemi, where she was known as Diana Nemorensis ("Diana of the Woods"); and the other at Capua under the name of Diana Tifatina (where she is the goddess of the crossroads and often associated with Hecate). In the eastern Empire her major shrine was at Ephesus, the temple of Artemis (one of the Seven Wonders of the ancient World) and the location of the well-known biblical reference where the mob shouted "Great is Diana of the Ephesians" against St. Paul's teachings (Acts 19,34). At Ephesus, Diana was represented with a great many breasts and other symbols linking her with **Cybele**.

The cult of Diana at Nemi, where she is often associated with Taurian Artemis, welcomed human sacrifices, and her priest—known as the Rex Nemorensis—could be replaced by whoever killed him (this forms a core element of Sir James Frazier's great study of anthropology *The Golden Bough*).

DIDO

Queen of Carthage and one of the tragic figures of classical mythology, best known from the account in Virgil's *Aeneid*. Her origins lie much further in Phoenician legend, where she is known as Elissa, daughter of Mutto, king of Tyre, and sister of Pygmalion. Pygmalion inherited the kingdom, but had Elissa's (Dido's) husband Sucharbas (the priest of Heracles) killed so that he could seize his wealth. Dido fled from Tyre with her adherents and, after making landfall in Cyprus, went on to Utica in North Africa. Here she was well received and, when she asked for land on which she and her party could settle, she was granted as much as could be covered by a bull's hide. She cut the hide into one very long thin strip with which she was able to enclose a large tract of land outside Carthage, now known as the Hill of Byrsa.

Two versions are given of Dido's death. The local king, Iarbas, wished to marry her but she had no liking for the match. In order to gain some time, she said that she needed three months to placate the spirit of her murdered husband Sicharbas. At the end of that time, she had a great funeral pyre built and committed suicide on it. The other story tells of **Aeneas** arriving at Carthage and being welcomed by the queen. When out hunting one day, they were overtaken by a storm and sought shelter in a cave where their love blossomed, a scene often depicted in Roman art. Iarbas called upon **Zeus** to remove the stranger who stood in his way, and Zeus, knowing that Aeneas was destined to found Rome, had him leave without even saying farewell to Dido. Learning that she had been abandoned, Dido committed suicide on a funeral pyre.

DIOMEDES

There are two characters by this name in Greek legend, one a hero of the Trojan War and one an unpleasant king of Thrace.

Dido, Queen of Carthage, greets Aeneas.

The hero of Troy was the son of Tydeus and Deipyle. His early history is very involved, but his major appearance is at Troy. There, he was the constant companion of **Odysseus** in all his exploits. Together they sought and found **Achilles** among the daughters of Lycomedes, persuaded **Agamemnon** to sacrifice **Iphigenia** for a favorable wind, stole the Palladium from the temple of **Athena** at Troy, and ambushed and killed the spy Dolan. Diomedes was a brave fighter who stood against both **Hector** and **Aeneas**, and also wounded **Ares** and **Aphrodite** when they became involved in the conflict.

It was said that Diomedes had one of the swiftest journeys back from the Trojan War, but when he got back to Argos he found that his wife, Aegiale, had been unfaithful to him (brought about by Aphrodite's malice at his having wounded her). She, rather like **Clytemnestra**, had plans to kill her husband, but he escaped and left Argos, making his way to southern Italy. There his prowess earned him the daughter of King Danus in marriage, but he later seems to have been killed by the king, and his companions turned into birds in their grief at his death.

DIONYSUS

Greek equivalent of **Bacchus**. Although a latecomer to the ranks of the 12 Olympian Gods, he had a huge and complex mythology built round him. Originally a wine god from Thrace, northern Greece, he soon found wide acceptance. He was the son of **Zeus** by the nymph **Semele**. **Hera**, in her jealousy, brought about the death of Semele, but Zeus was able to save the six-month-old unborn child to be born again from his thigh. To keep him out of harm's (Hera's) way, Dionysus was brought up by his aunt Ino and the nymphs of Nysa, but Hera learned of this and in vengeance sent Ino mad, while the nymphs became the constellation Hyades.

Dionysus met with many adventures as a young man. Lycurgus, king of Thrace, tried to take him prisoner, but Dionysus escaped by hiding beneath the sea with the sea nymph Thetis. The king was driven mad and, imagining that he was attacking the vine, the sacred tree of Dionysus, he proceeded to hack at it with an ax. In his confused state he chopped off his son's hands and feet and cut his own leg. When he recovered his senses he realized his kingdom had been struck sterile by the god. The only way Dionysus could be appeased, and the curse lifted, was by the death of Lycurgus. His people had him torn apart by attaching a horse to each of his limbs and driving them off in different directions.

Pirates who kidnapped Dionysus for ransom, not knowing who he was, jumped overboard in terror when he manifested himself and turned the ship's mast into a sprouting vine. They were turned into dolphins.

A major part of his mythology is concerned with his journey to India, a semi-religious and military conquest. His triumphal return, accompanied by frenzied scenes, is often featured in art, especially on Roman sarcophagi. The Dionysiac or Bacchic rout is a major feature of his cult and involved women running riot in a religious ecstasy. The god revenged himself on Pentheus, king of Thebes, who was against the introduction of the cult of Dionysus, by having the king's wife, Agave, literally tear him apart in her religious frenzy.

Once Dionysus' cult was recognized worldwide, he became a true god and

Dionysius, accompanied by a satyr.

Dionysius.

was accepted amongst the Olympians. It was after this that he found **Ariadne** asleep on Naxos and married her.

Music, dancing, and revelry were his hallmarks; his instruments, the cymbals and pipes; and his emblem, the thyrsus—a wine wand entwined in ivy. His adherents wore crowns of myrtle since the legend said that he had given that plant, of which he was very fond, to **Hades** in exchange for releasing his mother **Semele** from the Underworld.

DIOSCURI

The twin brothers Castor and Pollux were the sons of **Leda**, wife of King Tyndareus of Sparta, by **Zeus**. He visited her in the guise of a swan and her children, the twin boys and their sister **Helen**, were born from an egg. The Dioscuri were involved in contests with **Theseus** (who had carried off their sister Helen). They sailed with **Jason** and the **Argonauts** and were present at the Calydonian Boar Hunt.

According to one legend, they abused the laws of guest hospitality when they were invited to the wedding feast of Lynceus and Idas, who were marrying the daughters of Leucippus. Apparently the Dioscuri decided to carry off the two brides, and in the ensuing fight Castor was killed by Idas and Lycenus by Pollux. Zeus forthwith killed Idas with a thunderbolt and carried the wounded Pollux up to heaven. The brothers did not wish to be parted, Castor in the Underworld and Pollux in heaven, so Zeus allowed them to spend alternate days with the gods. Both were represented with horses, although Castor was the one skilled as a horseman and Pollux noted as a boxer. They subsequently became the constellation known as Gemini or The Twins. Because they had achieved divine status by the outbreak of the Trojan War, they were not involved, as one would expect, in the recovery of their sister Helen from **Paris** of Troy.

In Roman legend the Dioscuri fought on the Roman side at the battle of Lake Regillus against the Latins in 496 BC. After the battle they were seen watering their horses at the Spring of Juturna in the Roman Forum to announce their victory. A temple to them is located nearby.

DUMUZI

Important Sumerian shepherd-god, whose name is better known by the Hebrew form **Tammuz**, adopted as the name of the fourth month in the late Babylonian calendar, and still used as a month name in Hebrew and Arabic. The sources present a complexity of traditions about Dumuzi; he probably began as a historical figure (he is referred to in the Sumerian King List), but at some point his myth merged with that of the god Amaushumgalanna. Sumereian poetic texts attest to Dumuzi as the lover and husband of **Inanna** (see **Ishtar**), and in Inanna's Descent to the Netherworld he is sacrificed by her so that she may escape the clutches of the subterranean constabulary and return to Uruk. Dumuzi's death through Inanna also features in the story Dumuzi's Dream. He was certainly a figure of fertility. The fertility of Sumer was encouraged under, for example, the kings of the Ur III and Isin dynasties in an annual sacred ritual, in which the king enacted the role of Dumuzi and the high priestess that of Inanna. There is no evidence that Dumuzi is a vegetation god, and earlier attempts to see him as the forerunner of J.G. Frazer's "Dying God" who "annually died and rose again from the dead," are not all born out by cuneiform evidence.

E, F

EA

Also known as Eenki, the Sumerian Lord of the Earth or Underworld, the third most important god of the earlier Sumerian pantheon. Ea is the god of wisdom and magic, Lord of the Apsu, the cosmic sweet waters under the earth. Son of An, and brother to **Adad**, he is father of **Adapa** and Aslluhi (see **Marduk**), who appears with him in many incantations against evil. Marduk notices the symptoms in a patient and goes to tell his father what has happened. Ea invariably replies, "My son, what do you already not know? What can I add to you?" leaving Marduk to come up with a treatment from his own knowledge. His principal cult was located in the city of Eridu, where his temple was called Eabzu. Enki/Ea appears commonly in Mesopotamian myths, especially in Sumer, where he is always a good friend to mankind, but often unreliable and mischievous in his behavior to other gods. His symbol is a turtle.

ECHO

There are two characters of this name in classical mythology, both nymphs. One was unsuccessfully wooed by **Pan** and then torn to pieces by local shepherds, only her voice surviving. The other, better known, was a daughter of the Air and the earth-goddess Tellus, and an attendant on **Hera**. Hera deprived her of speech because her chatter prevented the goddess catching her husband **Zeus** in his amours with other nymphs. All poor Echo could do was repeat the last words spoken to her. She tried to make love to **Narcissus** with fragments of his own speech and, when he repulsed her, wasted away, only her voice remaining.

Europa abducted by Zeus in his bull manifestation.

ELECTRA

Daughter of the Greek king **Agamemnon** and **Clytemnestra**, a major figure in Greek tragedy and prominent in the ***Orestes*** cycle. There are several others of that name in mythology, but she is pre-eminent. After Agamemnon's return from Troy, and his murder by Aegisthus and Clytemnestra, Electra was herself saved only be the intercession of her mother, and then reduced to a servile condition, possibly even imprisoned in Mycenae. She saved her infant brother Orestes by smuggling him away to Strophus at Delphia, where he was brought up with Pylades, the son of the house, thus beginning their life-long friendship.

When her brother returned grown up, she recognized him at Agamemnon's tomb and incited him to kill their father's murderers. When he was subsequently pursued by the Erinyes (the **Furies**) for the double murder and matricide, she stood by him. Orestes gave her in marriage to his friend Pylades, who took her back to Phocis where they had two children: Medon and Strophius.

ENKIDU

In the Akkadian *Epic of* ***Gilgamesh***, Enkidu is the wild man of the beasts who, defeated by Gilgamesh, becomes his friend and companion. In the earlier Sumerian Gilgamesh poems Enkidu's status is, by contrast, that of a servant.

ENLIL

Lord Wind, one of the principal gods of the Mesopotamian pantheon, worshipped especially in his temple Ekur in the city of Nippur. His parentage is variously given as Anu, chief of the gods, or the primal gods Enki and Ninki (different from **Ea**/Enki). Many of the more important gods are described as his offspring, including **Ishtar/Inanna**, **Sin**/Nanna-Su'en, **Nergal**, **Ninurta**, Ningirsu (his prime son), and **Shamash**/Utu. His wife is usually Ninlil, although the grain-goddess Sud had this status in some contexts. He is praised above all as cosmic administrator and the power in the storm. In some mythological passages he is a creative benevolent god, but in the myth Enlil and Ninlil, he rapes the young Ninlil, thus begetting Nanna-Su'en, and is banished from Nippur to the Underworld as a sex criminal. He is followed by Ninlil and takes the form of three different men on the journey to lie with her again, each time engendering another Underworld deity. In the cuneiform Flood stories it is Enlil who takes the decision to destroy mankind.

EROS

The Greek god of love (his Roman equivalent being **Cupid**), usually represented as a small chubby winged child, was the son of **Aphrodite** by either **Zeus**, **Ares** or **Hermes**. There are numerous contradictions in the early legends and it is only later, mainly because of poetic writings, that he settles into the well-known form described. His attributes were a bow and a quiver full of arrows, the latter used to inflame love, as was the lighted torch he is sometimes shown wielding. He was always getting into scrapes, but was benevolently tolerated by the gods. He could be shown playing, throwing a quoit or driving a hoop. Sometimes he appears as a conqueror, with helmet on head and spear on shoulder. His power over both gods and men was indicated by showing him riding on a lion or dolphin, or breaking the thunderbolts of Zeus.

ETANA

Hero of the Etana myth, and a king of the First Dynasty of Kish, according to the Sumerian King List, ruling in the early third millennium BC. The myth as now recovered tells of Etana's wife being childless and dreaming of the "plant of birth," which her husband resolves to find for her. In the next scene there is a tree beside a river where an eagle and a serpent live harmoniously together as hunting partners. The eagle, however, treacherously consumes the serpent's young, so the serpent goes weeping to **Shamash** for help. The latter shows him a trick to get the eagle caught in a pit. Etana rescues the eagle, who—

in a famous episode that appears to be one of the few mythological passages convincingly recognized in the art of the cylinder seals—transports him up to Heaven on its back. In fact there seem to be several flights involved, and a sequence of dreams, but the outcome of the myth seems to be that Etana and his wife do get a son.

EUROPA

The daughter of Agenor, king of Phoenicia, and Telephassa. Her famous brother was **Cadmus**. She was a beautiful girl who caught the eye of **Zeus** one day while on the shore at Sidon (or Tyre). He transformed himself into a snow-white bull with crescent horns among the herds of Agenor, and lay down at her feet as she gathered flowers in the meadows with her attendants. Her initial fear being overcome, she stroked the animal and then climbed upon its back. Immediately, the bull headed for the sea and plunged in, making for Crete. Zeus took Europa to Gortyna in central Crete and there made love to her beneath a tree. This became part of the folklore of the area, even to the extent of a young girl in the branches being represented on the city's later coinage. Europa gave birth to three sons: **Minos**, Sarpedon (who became king of Lycia and was killed at Troy by **Patroclus**), and Rhadamanthys (a just king, who became one of the judges in Hades). From Zeus, Europa received three presents: the bronze man Talos who guarded the shores of Crete, a hunting spear that could never miss, and a dog that always ran its quarry down. Zeus then gave her in marriage to Asterion, king of Crete, who, since their marriage was childless, adopted Europa's three sons.

The subject of Europa and the Bull is a favorite one in classical and later European art. The bull subsequently became Taurus among the signs of the Zodiac, and Europa gave her name to the continent of Europe.

EURYDICE

In Greek myth the wife of **Orpheus**. While fleeing the unwelcome attentions of Aristaeus, a son of **Apollo**, she was bitten by a snake and died. The gods were angry with Aristaeus and destroyed all his bees. In atonement, to the shame of Eurydice, he sacrificed four bulls and four heifers, leaving their carcasses out to rot, at which swarms of bees returned to his land. Orpheus, however, in grief at his loss, made his way into the Underworld and so succeeded in charming **Hades** with the music of his lyre that he agreed to release Eurydice. There was one condition: her shade would follow him to the upper air as he played, but he must not look back until he had reached daylight. Almost there, he could not resist the temptation to glance behind and see if she really was following. Immediately the condition was broken and she was dragged back into the Underworld.

FURIES

In Greek mythology three goddesses who inflict the vengeance of the gods on those who wrongly shed blood. They are also called the Erinyes, which literally means "the kindly ones," presumably an attempt at appeasement. They were born from the drops of blood that flowed from the wound that **Saturn** inflicted on **Cronus**, and are envisaged as terrifying in appearance, wielding whips and torches and with serpents coiled in their hair. It is they who pursue **Orestes** after he has killed his mother, despite the fact that he acted in obedience to **Apollo**.

Hermes with Eurydice and Orpheus.

G

GAIA

The archetypal mother in classical mythology, one of the earliest of the primitive gods from whom all others sprang. She was born after Chaos in the primeval order and then, self-engendered, gave birth to **Uranus** (the sky), the Mountains, and Pontus (the sea). By Uranus she then bore six male and six female Titans, followed by three Cyclops (one-eyed giants), and three Hecatoncheires (violent 100-armed creatures). Uranus became very tyrannical and so Gaia persuaded **Cronus**, the youngest of the Titans who hated his father, to rid her of him. She gave him a sharp sickle and he castrated his father, throwing the testicles over his shoulder where the dripping blood resulted in Gaia giving birth to the three **Furies** (the Erinyes), the Giants (huge beings with serpents instead of legs), and the Ash Nymphs.

Ganymede.

Several of the early Greek poets, such as Hesiod, describe Gaia, although curiously she is not mentioned by Homer, where the gods concerned are all of the newer generation. Subsequently aspects of Gaia's role as Mother Earth were taken over by other goddesses, such as **Cybele** and **Demeter**, to whom various of the gods were allocated as their offspring.

GANYMEDE

In Greek myth a very beautiful youth, a son of the royal house of Troy. The legends vary as to who were his father and mother; generally, he was said to be the younger son of Tros and Callirhoe. **Zeus** saw the boy and wished to have him on Mount Olympus. One day, while Ganymede was guarding his father's flocks close to Troy, Zeus flew down in the shape of an eagle and carried him off to Mount Olympus. There he acted as cupbearer and was specially employed to pour the nectar that Zeus drank. The story was a favorite one in ancient art and is often found on vessels to do with

Geb, the earth, his wife Nut, the sky above him.

wine and also on mosaics; Ganymede, being lifted up by the eagle, can be found as far apart as the Roman villas at Bignor in Sussex and Paphos in Cyprus.

GEB

In Egyptian mythology the earth is envisaged as a god, contrasting with the Indo-European concept of the earth as a female principle. In the theogony of Heliopolis, the offspring of **Atum**—the god **Shu** and the goddess **Tefnut**—gave birth to Geb, the earth-god, and his sister-consort **Nut**, the sky-goddess. Geb is often depicted supine, raising himself slightly on one arm and inclining the other upward toward the sky. His most crucial role is in the transmission of kingship. It is the children of Geb and Nut who form the link between the cosmic deities and the throne of Egypt, often referred to as the "Throne of Geb," namely **Osiris**, **Isis**, **Set**, and **Nephthys**. Geb was a presiding judge over **Horus** and Set, the disputants for the throne of Egypt following the murder of Osiris. Geb's skin was shown as green, indicating the fruitfulness and fertility of the earth. It was thought that barley, a staple item of diet that provides both bread and beer, grew from the ribs of Geb.

GILGAMESH

King of the city of Uruk, and the hero of the *Epic of Gilgamesh*, the most important literary composition to survive from ancient Mesopotamia. The epic is best known from the Akkadian (Standard Babylonian) version on twelve cuneiform tablets, dating to the seventh century BC, although a cycle of Sumerian stories ("Gilgamesh and Huwawa", "Gilgamesh and the Bull of Heaven", "Gilgamesh and Akka", "Gilgamesh, **Enkidu** and the Netherworld", and "The Death of Gilgamesh") shows that the material derives from at least the second millennium BC and quite probably from the third.

The Standard Babylonian epic that is here summarized is still incomplete, and the story is partly known from earlier sources. It begins by praising

Gilgamesh, credited with composing the text himself, which was written on a stela and available in Uruk for all to read. Gilgamesh, two-thirds divine and one-third human, oppresses the young people of Uruk to the point that the goddess Aruru creates the wild man Enkidu to challenge him. Enkidu, born and raised among wild animals, is the direct antithesis of Gilgamesh, and their clash is inevitable. A trapper uses a harlot to seduce Enkidu, who has been freeing the animals caught in traps, and thereby reduces his natural powers. Enkidu then challenges Gilgamesh, who defeats him in a wrestling match, after which the two become intimate friends.

In a later episode, to counter the softening effect of their settled existence, Gilgamesh proposes a dangerous expedition to the Cedar Forest to defeat the formidable guardian **Humbaba**, long known by reputation and feared by the reluctant Enkidu, and to cut down the sacred Cedar Tree. Gilgamesh finally persuades him and the Uruk elders, and special weapons are made. On the six-day journey Gilgamesh enlists the help of **Shamash**, the sun god, and has a series of ominous dreams, which are expounded by Enkidu. Tensions between the two lead to a fight, but they persevere, and reach and enter the Cedar forest. After a battle Humbaba is defeated with the assistance of Shamash, who sends fierce winds to distract Humbaba. He is dispatched by a hesitant Gilgamesh, who keeps the head as a trophy. The heroes cut down the sacred Cedar and, building a raft from Humbaba's trees, sail back down the Euphrates to Uruk.

Once returned, Gilgamesh, is beset with other problems. The goddess **Ishtar** attempts to seduce and wed him, but he spurns her with a scornful reference to her ill-fated earlier lovers and she is roused to fury. She persuades her father Anu to send the Bull of Heaven against Uruk, regardless of the consequences. Many of the population lose their lives in pits made by the Bull before Gilgamesh kills it with his sword, then hurls its thigh in Ishtar's face. Enkidu then has a dream from which it emerges that his part in these feats requires punishment by death. Despite his protestations, Enkidu succumbs after a decline of 12 days, accusing Gilgamesh of having abandoned him. Gilgamesh mourns his friend profoundly, ordering a statue to be made. Realizing in his grief that one day he too will have to die, Gilgamesh turns to the pursuit of eternal life. He determines to gain the secret from **Utanapishtim**, the only man to have achieved immortality for his part in saving life from the flood. Gilgamesh starts on a journey to the Mouth of the Rivers to see him. The scorpion man and his mate attempt to dissuade him from the journey, as does Siduri, the tavern-keeper, who points to the folly of his search in one of the most powerful and affecting passages in cuneiform. Gilgamesh finds Urshanabi, the Ferryman, who instructs him how to cross with safety the Waters of Death. Armed with punting poles they cross and Gilgamesh meets Utanapishtim, who tells him the full story of the Flood, and how he rescued his family and all the beasts and animals of the field. This, the 11th tablet of the series, has provided the closest parallel to the flood narrative in Genesis. After further difficulties, Gilgamesh is shown how to gain the Plant of Eternal Youth. But, while he bathes in a spring, a snake steals and eats it, immediately sloughing off its old skin. Gilgamesh then resolves to return empty-handed to Uruk. It is often considered that this point marks the end of the original narrative, but there is also a 12th tablet, in which Enkidu goes down into the Underworld to rescue two objects that have been lost there, when he himself becomes trapped. Gilgamesh summons his ghost to ask about the conditions in the land beyond the grave. This tablet is a direct translation from the Sumerian "Gilgamesh, Enkidu and the Netherworld" and is regarded by many as an artificial appendage to the 11-tablet series.

GORGONS (See MEDUSA)

These were three sisters, Stheno, Eurale, and **Medusa**, who were the daughters of the sea gods Phorcys and Ceto. The first two of the sisters were immortal, but the third, Medusa, was mortal, and she is the one who is best known and most often referred to as the Gorgon, as if there were only one. The sisters lived in the far west, close by the Kingdom of the Dead. They were of frightful aspect with snakes entwined in their hair, hands of brass (or bronze), teeth as long as boar's tusks, bodies covered with impenetrable scales, and wings of gold. Their glance was so terrible that it turned the beholder to stone. Only **Poseidon**, of all the gods and men, was not afraid of them, and he fathered the giant Chrysaor and the winged horse **Pegasus** on Medusa. It was the hero **Perseus** who finally killed her.

The snake-haired Gorgon, Medusa.

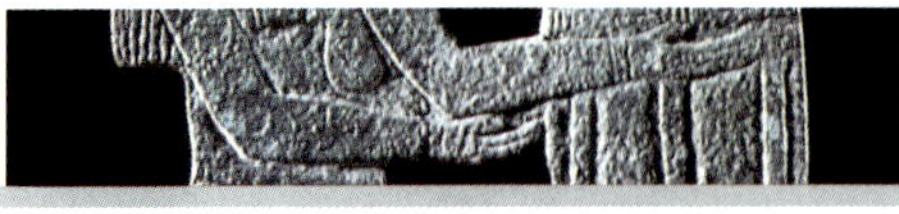

H

HADES

The god of the dead in classical mythology, known to the Romans as **Pluto**. Unlike similar deities in other religions, he was seen as a pitiless and frightening god. Hades was the son of **Cronus** and Rhea, and therefore the brother of **Zeus**. In the great division of the world after the defeat of the Titans, Hades was given Hell—or Tartarus—as his share, while Zeus took the earth and heavens, and **Poseidon** the sea.

Hades wanted a wife and he cast his eyes on **Persephone**, his niece, the young daughter of Zeus and **Demeter**. Her parents would have none of the match (although Zeus appears to have connived at subsequent events). Hades therefore took matters into his own hands. He kidnapped the girl one day while she was out picking flowers with other young girls in the plains of Sicily, and took her down into the Underworld. The gods were angry and Demeter mourned her daughter, causing the earth to be barren, in other words winter. Hades was told to restore the girl to her mother, but he had foreseen this and had given Persephone the seed of a pomegranate to eat. Anyone who had eaten anything in the Underworld could not return to the earth to live. A compromise was reached; Persephone would spend a third of the year in the Underworld with Hades as his wife, but she could return to earth the rest of the time. Demeter was satisfied with this, and Persephone, upon her return each year from below ground, personified the Spring, renewal, just as flowers and seeds pushed their way up through the earth at that season.

Hapy, personification of the Nile.

HAPY

Personification in Egyptian mythology of the Nile flood, one that has, with the advent of modern dams, now vanished from present-day Egypt. In pharaonic times, the increase in the speed and volume of the river was eagerly awaited—the fields would be refreshed and a new layer of fertile silt, carried all the way

Hades. Lord of the underworld, with his wife Persephone.

from Ethiopia, would be the basis of a rich harvest. Hapy lived in the caverns in the vicinity of the first cataract, possessing an androgynous body, pendulous breasts, and a swollen paunch, to indicate the fecundity brought to Egypt by the flood. His crown was often a clump of papyrus, which once grew in abundance by the Nile.

HATHOR

In Egyptian mythology the goddess Hathor is a complex deity. As a cow goddess the aspect of the universal mother predominates, but does not eclipse her role as symbolic consort of the pharaoh by virtue of being the wife of the royal hawk-god, **Horus**. There are three major forms under which Hathor, daughter of the sun god **Re**, can appear in the ancient iconography. Firstly, she can be depicted as an elegant woman wearing a crown of cow-horns with the sun disk between them. Secondly, she can assume the total body of a cow, often in this form suckling the young monarch with her udder of divine milk. Thirdly, in architectural elements her face is human, but her ears are bovine. It was a natural step for Greeks to equate

Hathor.

Hathor with **Aphrodite**. She was a goddess of sexual love, of joy, of music, and of dance. Love poetry in Egypt abounds with allusions to her as the "Golden One." In the story of the struggle between Horus and **Set** for the throne, when her father, the sun-god Re, retires in a sulk after a fight, it is Hathor who brings him back into the proceedings by going to him and displaying the intimate parts of her body.

HECTOR

Foremost of the Trojan warriors and the eldest son of **Priam**, king of Troy, and his wife Hecuba. He was married to Andromache, daughter of King Aetion of Thebes in Mysia (which town had been sacked by **Achilles** in the ninth year of the Trojan War, and Andromache's father and seven brothers had been killed). Hector and Andromache had a son called Astyanax.

In the *Iliad,* which is only concerned with the 10th and final year of the Trojan War, Hector plays a very prominent role. Whenever Achilles is not present on the Greek side, everyone falls before Hector. **Agamemnon** had wanted Hector killed from the outset, because he knew that the Greeks could never win while he lived. Many of Hector's exploits are noted in the legends and also often illustrated in Greek vase-paintings, notably his day-long fight with **Ajax**, at the end of which both combatants retired and sent each other presents.

The attack on the Greek ships, planned and led by Hector, was perhaps his greatest exploit. The Greeks were hard pressed and Achilles refused to leave his tent where he was sulking. **Patroclus**, Achilles' close friend, in an endeavor to turn the tide of battle, donned the armor of his friend and fought as him, but was killed by Hector. This at last brought Achilles to his senses and he emerged into the fray seeking revenge. Hector's destiny was to die at the hands of Achilles, and so no matter what the gods did to assist him, his life could only be prolonged and not saved. The petty jealousies and favoritisms of the gods played quite a part in this. **Athena** took the form of Hector's favorite brother, Delphobus, and urged him to stand against Achilles, promising to help him. Eventually Hector and Achilles met outside the Scean gate; Athena disappeared and Hector knew his fate was sealed. **Apollo** and **Ares**, his supporters till then, also deserted him. Hector was struck down and, as he lay dying, he entreated Achilles to return his body to his father, Priam. But Achilles refused, and Hector then foretold the imminent death of Achilles.

Achilles treated Hector's corpse abominably, piercing the heels, passing

Hector fighting Ajax.

a leather thong through them, and then dragging it around the walls of Troy in revenge for the death of Patroclus. The body was then left exposed in the Greek camp. Achilles refused all appeals for clemency or offer of ransom until the gods were so repelled by his actions that **Zeus** sent Iris to order him to release Hector's body for decent burial. For a large sum he then ransomed the body to Priam, and subsequently Hector's 12-day long funeral rites were performed under a truce.

HELEN

Greek princess who has become the epitome of female beauty. She was the cause of the Trojan War ("the face that launched a thousand ships and burnt the topless towers of Ilium," as Christopher Marlowe wrote). Helen's legend is extremely complicated, especially as recorded by ancient writers after Homer. She was the daughter of **Zeus** by **Leda**, whom he visited as a swan. Leda subsequently produced an egg from which were born Helen and her twin brothers the **Dioscuri** Castor and Pollux. Her mortal sister (the daughter of Tyndareus and Leda) was **Clytemnestra**.

From an early age Helen's beauty attracted many suitors. She was carried off by **Theseus** before the age of 10, and rescued by her twin brothers. Tyndareus, her mortal father, was very concerned by the number of her suitors, given variously from 29 to 99. He realized that by choosing Helen's husband, he would offend her other suitors, and conflict would follow. The wily **Odysseus** suggested a clever solution: the suitors were all sworn to accept Helen's choice and to support him should the need ever arise. She chose **Menelaus**, king of Sparta, and it was this oath that Menelaus invoked after her abduction by **Paris**. Odysseus was rewarded with the hand in marriage of **Penelope**, Tyndareus' niece. Helen and Menelaus had a daughter, Hermione.

Aphrodite had promised Paris the most beautiful woman in the world if she herself was awarded the Apple of Discord in his judgement between herself, **Hera** and **Athena**. She won the contest and Paris, on a visit to the Spartan court, seduced Helen and took her, together with a vast treasure and her slaves, away to Troy. Menelaus then invoked the oath and the support of the other princes and thus the Trojan War was set in motion.

At Troy Helen was looked upon as the wife of Paris, but she was disliked by the Trojans who saw her as the cause of their misfortunes. Only **Hector** and **Priam** realized that the will of the gods was being carried out, and that she was an innocent victim of that will. Although in sympathy with the Greeks, Helen, while at Troy, would stand on the walls and identify the Greek leaders for the Trojans; yet it was also said that she twice recognized Odysseus when he entered Troy in disguise and did not give him away. On the second occasion she actively assisted him when he and **Diomedes** stole the Palladium.

When Troy fell to the stratagem of the Wooden Horse, Helen took refuge in the sanctuary of **Apollo**, where her vengeful husband Menelaus found her and forgave her. Their return home to Sparta took eight years, and like that of Odysseus was beset by misfortune. Various versions of her death are given. Homer said that she became the epitome of the virtuous wife and was subsequently deified, along with Menelaus her husband, apparently at her request in recompense for all the wrongs she had done him. Another account has her enjoying eternal life with **Achilles**, her fourth husband in some legends on an island in the Euxine sea. Several variant stories have revenge as the theme of her death: she hanged herself in remorse, she was offered in sacrifice in Tauris, or she was killed by Thetis, the mother of Achilles, for having been the indirect cause of his death. Five heroes are associated with her as "husbands:" Theseus, Menelaus, Paris, Achilles, and Deophobus (after the death of his brother, Paris).

HEPHAESTUS

The Greek smith god, son of **Zeus** and **Hera**. He is always portrayed clad in a leather apron and as being lame. It was said that his lameness came about because he took his mother's part on Olympus in an argument with his father Zeus. In anger Zeus threw him from Olympus and he fell for a whole day before landing on the island of Lemnos, thus causing his deformity. Another version says that he was born deformed and Hera threw him into the sea in disgust. He lived in a cave on Lemnos for nine years and learnt the secrets of metalworking. Volcanoes were his workshops and his creations were masterpieces. It was to Hephaestus that Thetis turned when she wanted the finest armor made for her son **Achilles**. He also forged Zeus' thunderbolts.

Zeus married Hephaestus to **Aphrodite**, but she was unfaithful to him with **Ares**. Helios, the sun god, saw the two lovers together one day and told Hephaestus. He made an invisible net that could not be broken and strung it about Aphrodite's bed. When she was with her lover he sprang the trap and then called all the gods to see the pair enmeshed. When he released them, Aphrodite hid herself in shame.

Hephaestus.

Hera, long suffering wife of Zeus.

HERA

In Greek myth the long-suffering and at times spiteful wife of **Zeus**, the daughter of **Cronus** and Rhea and therefore also Zeus' sister. She was violently jealous of her husband's liaisons with various mistresses and often tried to bring about their harm, or even death, or pursued their children. She caused the death of **Semele**, the mother of **Dionysus**, and urged others to appalling deeds in her vindictiveness. At times she went too far and Zeus intervened, as when she endeavored to shipwreck **Heracles** upon his return from Troy. Zeus had her hung by the wrists from Olympus with an anvil tied to each foot. She is also credited with having instigated Heracles' Twelve Labors as a punishment.

Several places are suggested as to where Zeus married Hera, including the Gardens of the Hesperides, but the pair are generally associated with Crete (where Zeus was brought up on Mount Ida) and with the area of Knossos (where Hera's head appeared on some of the ancient coins). Zeus and Hera had four children: **Ares**, **Hephaestus**, Eileithyia and Hebe, the last two being goddesses of childbirth and youth respectively.

The major sanctuary of Zeus was at Olympia (where his chryselephantine statue by Pheidas was one of the Seven Wonders of the Ancient World), and Hera also had a temple alongside it. Her major shrine, however, was located in the plain of Argos and known as the Argive Heraion. It had a famous cult statue of her by the sculptor Polycleitos.

It was again in revenge, because she had lost the beauty contest judged by **Paris**, that Hera sided with the Greeks in the Trojan War. She was the especial protectress of **Achilles**, more so since she had brought up his mother, Thetis.

HERACLES

In Greek legend, Heracles (Roman name Hercules) is the greatest of the heroes of classical mythology. He was the son of **Zeus** by a Theban girl, Alcmena, and his conception is supposed to have taken three days and three nights to accomplish. Zeus' wife, **Hera**, singled out Heracles from among Zeus' many progeny as the focus of her anger and resentment, sending two snakes to destroy him when he was just a baby of eight months (the infant hero easily strangled the snakes). In early manhood he destroyed the lion of Mount Cithaeron and delivered his country from the annual tribute of 100 oxen, but he was driven mad by Hera and killed his own family in a frenzy. To expiate this crime, the famous Twelve Labors were imposed upon him by Eurystheus, king of Mycenae. These were: the killing of the Nemean lion, which he did with his bare hands, subsequently wearing the skin as a cloak; the destruction of the seven-headed hydra, a creature sacred to Hera; the capture of the Arcadian stag; the capture

Heracles defeats a centaur.

Heracles overcomes Cerebus.

of the Erymanthian boar, a creature that frightened Eurystheus so much that he hid in a storage jar for several days, a scene often depicted in Greek vase painting; the cleaning of the Augean stables, where 3000 oxen had been kept for many years; the killing of the carnivorous Stymphalian birds; the capture of the bull that **Poseidon** had sent to ravage Crete; the capture of the meat-eating mares of **Diomedes**; the stealing of the girdle of **Hippolyta**, queen of the Amazons; the killing of the monster Geryon and the capture of his flocks; bringing the apples from the Garden of the Hesperides, who guarded the fruit that **Gaia** gave to Hera on her marriage to Zeus, and fetching the three-headed hound **Cerberus** from the Underworld. He subsequently married Deianira, who unwittingly brought about his death by giving him a poisoned tunic to wear.

HERMES

In Greek mythology the messenger of the gods, son of **Zeus** and the nymph Maia; his Roman equivalent is **Mercury**. He also had the role of escorting the dead to the Underworld, and later became identified with the Norse god Odin, in his aspect of father of the slain. Hermes was also the patron of merchants and seamen, of good luck, and of thieves and pickpockets. He was renowned for his mischief-making. On the day after his birth, he stole the oxen of Admetus, which **Apollo** was guarding, and is credited with the invention of the lyre, which he gave the irate god as a peace-offering. Zeus often used him as an intermediary in his various amours, and gave him as a reward a winged helmet and sandals with which he is usually represented and which he lent to **Perseus**. In another aspect, Hermes was god of roads and of fertility, as repre-

Hermes, messenger of the gods.

sented by wayside shrines or hermeia, which were quadrangular pillars with a bust of the god on top and a phallus carved below.

HERYSHAF

In Egyptian mythology, an ancient ram-god particularly worshipped at a site called Henes not too far from modern Berisuef in Middle Egypt. The identification of Heryshaf with **Heracles** by the Greeks led to this cult center and city becoming known as Herakleopolis. The symbolism inherent in the name Heryshaf, which means "he who is upon his lake," is clearly that of a primeval deity emerging out of the watery chaos at the beginning of time. Heryshaf was envisaged as a universal sovereign "King of the Two Lands." Also he became a form of sun god and the northern breeze of his nostrils adds the notion of a creator deity to the solar imagery.

HIPPOLYTA

Queen of the Amazons and a warrior maiden, who was given in marriage to **Theseus** by **Heracles** after he had conquered her and removed her girdle as one of his Twelve Labors. In another version, Theseus falls in love with Hippolyta and throws down his sword in battle against her.

HIPPOLYTUS

Son of **Hippolyta** and **Theseus**. After the death of his mother, Theseus married Phaedra, who fell in love with her stepson, Hippolytus, and tried to seduce him. He resisted her advances, so infuriating her that she told Theseus that he had raped her. Theseus, in anger, asked **Poseidon** to punish his son, and Poseidon sent a sea monster, which so terrified Hippolytus' horses as he fled in his chariot along the seashore that they bolted among the rocks and Hippolytus was killed.

HOPE

There exist various interpretations of Hope, who was the only thing that remained in the box after **Pandora**'s curiosity got the better of her.

HORATIUS

Legendary hero of ancient Rome who, together with two companions, defended the Sublican bridge across the River Tiber against the army of the Etruscans led by Lars Porsena, while the Romans destroyed the bridge so that the Etruscans could not cross. His two companions jumped to safety before the bridge fell, but Horatius remained on the far side and then jumped with all his weapons into the Tiber, commending his life to the god of the river. The river duly bore him up and delivered him safely on the Roman side, and Horatius was given as a reward as much land as he could plough in a day.

HORUS

The Egyptian hawk-god Horus is exceptionally complicated to analyze since he is a deity of the distant sky in his solar aspect and yet immediate and present among Egyptians in his manifestation of the pharaoh. The name Horus means "The One Far-off" or "He on High." Representations show Horus both wholly in the form of a hawk as early as the late Predynastic Period just prior to 3000 BC, and human to the shoulders with the head of a hawk. The iconography of the hawk itself symbolized the sky with its wings and the sun and moon with its two eyes. A ubiquitous motif in Egyptian architecture and relief is that of a winged sun-disk. This, too, is Horus as "He of Behdet" (a sanctuary in the

Hope.

Horus, wearing the crown of Upper Egypt.

north-east Delta), and announces without need of explanatory text that the hawk propels the sun-disk across the heavens. As Horakte he subsumed under his identity the Great **Sphinx** at Giza, originally constructed in the image of Pharaoh Khafre (2520–2494 BC) as a human-headed lion guarding the causeway leading to the king's pyramid.

The other side to Horus is his role in the myth of the transmission of the throne of Egypt. His mother was the goddess **Isis** who conceived him by magical power from the body of his murdered father, **Osiris**. His name Harsiese means just "Horus Son of Isis." When he reached maturity as Haroeris or "Horus the Elder" he was able to make his bid for the throne, occupied by the usurper **Set**. The richest source of information on the struggle of Horus against Set can be found in a racy, even scandalous, account surviving on papyrus in the British Museum, written about 1150 BC. The opening scenes are set in a tribunal established to decide on the legality of the rival claims of Horus and Set. Set is supported by the sun-god **Re**, as being entitled to throne by virtue of being the older. Horus and Set engage in a series of contests to prove their claims. In one episode Set feigns reconciliation with Horus, but then makes a homosexual attack on him. Horus foils this attack without Set realizing, and collects Set's semen. Isis throws it into the marshes and spreads some of the semen of Horus himself on a bed of lettuces, Set's favorite food, which he predictably eats. The result is that when Set tries to humiliate Horus as a result of sexually assaulting him, his semen, which he believed was in Horus, is found to answer him from the marshes. In fact it is Set who is humiliated because the semen of Horus emerges from his head. Another contest sees Horus and Set change into hippopotami to endure three months submergence under water.

Eventually the award of the kingship is given to Horus, which means that the pharaoh, regarded as a living manifestation of the god, legitimately rules Egypt by virtue of the verdict of the divine tribunal. We are left in no doubt about the identification between the monarch and Horus when we admire the majestic diorite statue of Khafre in Cairo Museum, where the hawk-god spreads his wings protectively behind the royal headcloth. Finally, the god permeates Egyptian iconography and funerary and temple inscriptions in the most powerful amuletic symbol known as the "Wadjat Eye" or "Eye of Horus." In one episode of the contest for the throne, Set gouged out Horus' eyes, leaving him vulnerable. **Hathor** rubbed Horus with milk of a gazelle which restored his sight. The imagery of the "Sound Eye" (Wadjat in Egyptian) is a puissant sign of protection and perfection, and takes the form of a human eye with a cosmetic line and eyebrow, with the feathered marking of a hawk's cheek below it.

HUMBABA

(Sumerian Huwawa), the guardian of the Cedar Forest appointed by **Enlil**, whom **Gilgamesh** and **Enkidu** defeated together in the *Epic of Gilgamesh*. It is clear from representations on cylinder seals depicting this scene that the terrifying Humbaba was human in body with lion's claws, a distorted staring face, and much hair. Clay models, probably prepared for teaching purposes, depict Humbaba's face, which is likened to a sheep's intestines.

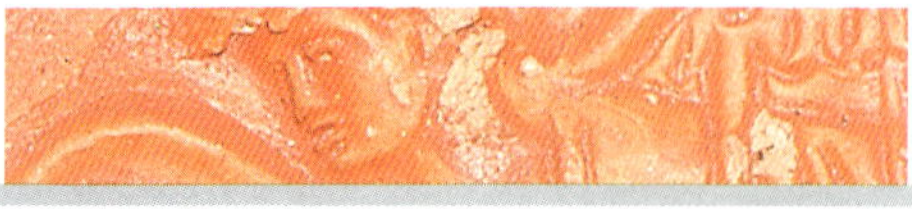

I

ICARUS

Son of **Daedalus** in Greek myth who, with his father, fled from Crete on wings made of wax and feathers to escape the wrath of **Minos**. Daedalus arrived safely in Attica, but Icarus in his pride flew too close to the sun, which melted the wax in his wings so that he fell into the sea and was drowned.

IMDUGED (See ANZU)

Icarus falling.

Icarus and Daedalus escape from Crete.

Imhotep, designer of the first pyramid.

IMHOTEP

The most important example of an ancient Egyptian official gaining such fame and prestige that eventually he became deified. He is historically attested as the vizier of King Netjerykhet, or Djoser (2630–2611 BC), for whom the Step Pyramid at Saqqara was built. Imhotep was the architect of this pyramid, which was the first large-scale stone monument ever constructed in the world. He was given the privilege of having his name and titles carved on the pedestal of a statue of the pharaoh. By the Ptolemaic era Imhotep was deified and worshipped as a god from Saqqara to the temple of **Isis** at Philae. His reputation in medicine as a healer led to a natural identification between him and the Greek god **Ascelpius**.

INANNA (See ISHTAR)

Jupiter and Io.

IO

In Greek myth a priestess of **Hera** at Argos. **Zeus** fell in love with her and visited her disguised as cloud of mist. The jealous Hera surprised them together and, to save his mistress, Zeus changed her into a beautiful heifer. Hera then persuaded Zeus to give her the heifer as a gift, and set the 100-eyed Argus to watch her, but Zeus sent **Hermes** to destroy Argus and release Io, still in heifer form. She reached Egypt, pursued by Hera's jealousy, where Zeus restored her to her human form. In one version she then married **Osiris** and was worshipped under the name of **Isis**.

IPHIGENIA

In Greek legend daughter of **Agamemnon**, high-king of Greece, and his wife **Clytemnestra**. When the Greek fleet was ready to set sail for Troy in order to rescue **Helen**, they were delayed at Aulis by contrary winds. The goddess **Artemis** was angry with Agamemnon for killing her favorite stag, and only the sacrifice of Iphigenia would appease her and cause the wind to change. At first Agamemnon refused, and ordered all the Greeks to return to their homes, but he was finally persuaded to consent. Iphigenia was summoned to Aulis on the pretext of marriage to **Achilles** and all was prepared for the sacrifice. At the last moment Artemis took pity on the girl and substituted a stag, bearing Iphigenia off to be her priestess at Taurica, where she was charged with sacrificing all strangers to the goddess. This she did until she recognized her brother, **Orestes**, as one of the potential victims. She revealed herself to him and they fled together.

ISHKUR (See ADAD)

ISHTAR

The most important of all the Mesopotamian goddesses, and a multi-faceted personality, occurring in cuneiform texts of all periods. Her Sumerian name is **Inanna**, which probably means "Lady of Heaven," and her Akkadian name, Ishtar, is related to the Syrian Astarte and the biblical Ashtaroth. Ishtar is usually considered as a daughter of **Anzu**, with her cult located at Uruk, but there are other traditions as to her ancestry, and it is probable that these reflect originally different goddesses that were identified with her. Ishtar is the subject of a cycle of texts describing her love affair and ultimately fatal relationship with **Tammuz**. She is also generally the goddess of love and sex, and textual evidence exists to indicate her connection with prostitution. She is important as a goddess of war, who accompanies kings in battle, ablaze with excitement. Ishtar is also known to be the planet **Venus**. Her early symbol was a reed bundle.

ISIS

Egyptian goddess whose two major characteristics were her magical powers and her link with the throne of Egypt as the symbolic mother of the pharaoh. Isis can be shown wearing the symbol of the throne or the headdress of cow-horns and the sun disk. Her genealogy was the same as that of **Osiris**, to whom she was both a sister and a wife, in that she was the child of **Geb** and **Nut**. In a Golden Age she ruled over Egypt at Osiris' side. When Osiris was murdered by **Set**, she sought out his body and with her wings revived him sufficiently to become pregnant with **Horus**, whom she brought up safely in the Delta marshes, guarding him from the threat of Set. She protected him against scorpions, snakes, and fevers, and was consequently involved whenever a child suffered from poisonous bites or fever. Magical spells survive to show that a sick child was identified with Horus so that the magic of Isis could cure the ailment.

The magic of Isis was powerful enough to cajole the sun-god **Re** into revealing his secret name. This knowledge gave the person aware of it power over the bearer of that name. She caught some of the saliva dribbled to earth by the sun-god and mixed it with clay to form a serpent, which in turn stung the god, who became seriously ill with his own poison. Isis, summoned to effect a cure, refused unless Re revealed his secret name.

The sun-god prevaricated and reeled off a list of names and epithets, but Isis realized that his secret name was not included. The poison burned more intensely and, at last, Re, binding Isis by an oath not to divulge his secret name any further than to her son Horus, revealed the powerful knowledge to the goddess.

In the Hellenistic and Roman period, the cult of Isis took on a new form as a mystery religion. Some of its rituals were revealed in paintings at Pompeii and Herculaneum, and also in *The Golden Ass* of Apuleius, a Roman north African writer of the second century AD. Her temples spread across the Mediterranean to the Acropolis at Athens and to the island of Delos. In Egypt itself, the temple of Isis on the island of Philae, just south of the first cataract of the Nile at Aswan, was the last to hold out against the advent of Christianity, not being surpassed until the reign of the sixth century Byzantine emperor Justinian.

The great mother goddess Isis.

J

JANUS

A legendary king who was reputed to be the first ruler of Italy. He founded a small town on the River Tiber, which he called Janiculum, still the name of one of the seven hills of Rome. During his reign, **Saturn** fled to Italy, driven from heaven by his son **Jupiter**, and Janus welcomed him and made him co-ruler. He is represented with two faces looking in opposite directions, because he knew both past and future. His double-gated temple in the forum in Rome had an additional significance: the gates opened in time of war. Janus later developed into a god of all beginnings; the month January was sacred to him, while as four-headed Janus, or Janus Quadrifons, he presided over the four seasons.

Juno.

JASON

Son of Aeson and the leader of the **Argonauts**. When Aeson's father, Cretheus, died, Aeson's half-brother, Pelias—son of **Poseidon** and Cretheus' wife Tyro, usurped the throne, allowing Aeson to live in Iolcos as a private citizen. Not trusting Pelias, Jason's parents smuggled him out of Iolcos under cover of a mock funeral and a report of his death, and gave him to the Centaur **Chiron** to be reared in his care. Meanwhile Pelias was warned by the Delphic oracle to beware of a descendant of Aelus (Jason's great-grandfather, who would appear wearing only one sandal).

When he reached manhood, Jason left Mount Pelion (where the Centaur lived) and returned to Iolcos, strangely dressed in a tiger skin and with a lance in each hand. Thus attired, he arrived in the main square of Iolcos just as Pelias was offering a sacrifice. Significantly, Jason was wearing only one sandal, the other having been lost when he helped an old lady (**Hera**, who hated Pelias for his neglect of her rites) to cross the River Anauros.

Pelias was alarmed at Jason's return. When, on the sixth day, Jason claimed the power that was his by right, Pelias ordered him to bring the fleece of the ram that had magically carried Phrixus, son of Creutheus' brother, Athamas, to Colchis. Pelias was certain that Jason would not return since the Golden Fleece was guarded by a dragon. In return for the fleece, Pelias agreed to name Jason his successor. This was a clever move because he was caught in a dilemma: on the one hand he could not harm the young man during festival time, especially as he probably enjoyed the support of many people, and on the other hand he represented a serious threat not only to Pelias' throne but also to his life.

Jason consulted the Delphic oracle and gathered round him a band of the noblest heroes in Greece, the **Argonauts**, some of whom had been boyhood friends on Mount Pelion. Besides **Heracles** there were specialists such as Argos the shipbuilder, Tiphys the pilot, Lynceus who had marvelous eyesight, **Orpheus** with the magical powers of his music, and Polydeuces the boxer. The witch **Medea**, Aeetes' daughter, gave Jason indispensable help in winning the Golden Fleece and when he returned from Colchis, he married her and gave the fleece to Pelias. At this point the traditions diverge dramatically, some saying that Jason ruled instead of Pelias, and some that he lived quietly at Iolcos. One story is that Medea by her magic caused the death of Pelias, persuading his daughters to boil him in a cauldron on the grounds that this would rejuvenate him, which of course it did not.

With Pelias' death, Jason and Medea were driven from Iolcos by Pelias' son. After 10 years together in Corinth, Jason transferred his affections from Medea to Glauce, daughter of King Creon. Medea murdered the two children she had by Jason and fled into the sky in a chariot. Jason met his death when part of the stern of the Argo fell on him whilst he was sleeping.

JUNO

A Roman goddess of marriage and the long-suffering wife of **Jupiter**. Like her Greek equivalent, **Hera**, she was protec-

The three gods of the Capitol at Rome: Minerva, Jupiter and Juno.

Jupiter armed with a thunderbolt.

tor of women, in particular married women. A festival took place in her honor on the calends (first) of March. When referred to as Juno Lucina she was the goddess of childbirth. Those making offerings to her had to untie any knots about their person, since these could hinder a safe delivery. As Juno Moneta she governed finance, and the Roman mint was located in her temple on the Capitoline Hill. Juno's name is the feminine counterpart of Jupiter (Heavenly Father) and, whereas all men had their "Genius," all women had their "Juno."

JUPITER

The Roman equivalent of **Zeus**, he came to hold the predominant position in the Roman pantheon, appearing as the god of the sky, of daylight, of the weather, and, particularly, of thunder and lightning. He came to hold this position partly through his identification with Zeus and partly through the assistance he offered **Romulus** in driving back the Sabines. Romulus established a temple to Jupiter at the spot where he had first implored his assistance. With his temple on the Capitol, Jupiter was seen as the supreme power whose priest (Flamen Dialis) was married to the priestess of **Juno** (flaminca). It was to Jupiter that newly-elected consuls offered their first prayers, and it was he who oversaw international relations through the mediation of the college of priests. The establishment of a Capitol, similar to that at Rome, in every provincial city affirmed the political bond between Rome as mother city and the daughters that were all a copy of her blueprint

K

KHEPRI

In Egyptian mythology the scarab beetle was a form of sun-god synonymous with the idea of ancient Egypt itself, representing the sun at dawn emerging above the mountains of the eastern horizon. The ancient Egyptians observed that scarab beetles pushed around huge balls of dung and dirt, and so made the analogy that the sun in the sky could be propelled across the firmament by a gigantic scarab beetle. They also observed that from the ball a young scarab emerged spontaneously, a fitting image for a creator-god who arose out of the primeval water self-generated, hence the name Khepri or "He who is coming into being." Jewelry from ancient Egypt often included a scarab carved out of semi-precious stones.

KHNUM

In Egyptian mythology the ram-god Khnum was a creator-god who molded the human race on a potter's wheel. In a hymn from his cult temple at Esna, which reads like an anatomy lesson, every part of a human being owes its existence to Khnum's expertise. He was in addition an important god presiding over the Cataract regions of the Nile. It was at his behest that **Hapy**, the god of the Inundation, rose from his caverns at Aswan.

KHONSU

In Egyptian mythology the moon-god, child of the union of **Amun-Re** and **Mut** at Thebes. His name means "wanderer" and refers to the most erratic cycle of the moon in the sky when compared to the course of the sun-god. Khonsu could be hawk-headed or take the form of a child wearing the sidelock of youth, and he wore a crown showing the disk of the full moon resting between the horns of the crescent moon. Khonsu played an integral part in the New Year celebrations at Thebes, when his statue accompanied those of his parents to the temple of Luxor, leaving its normal abode in his temple just to the south of Amun's at Karnak. He also had a manifestation as a god of healing and exorcism. In the reign of Rameses II (1290–1224 BC), his statue was transported from Thebes to Bakhtar to drive out a malevolent spirit from the princess Bentresh, and was only returned to Thebes after four years.

Moon god Khonsu.

L

LACHESIS

One of the Greek Fates (Moirai) represented from the time of Homer as three old women spinning out men's destinies like thread. The three were called **Clotho** ("the spinner"), who held the distaff, Lachesis ("the apportioner"), who drew off the thread, and **Atropos** ("the inflexible") who cut it short. A person's apportionment may govern what happens to him in life, but most often refers to his death, since death is everyone's portion. In mythology, the Fates played little part. Their relationship with the gods is variable. Thus they aided **Zeus** in his battles both against the giants and against Typhon. They persuaded the latter, when he was already under pressure from Zeus, to eat a diet of human food, assuring him, contrary to the truth, that it would strengthen him. **Apollo**, on the other hand, cheated the Fates, making them drunk, so allowing his friend Admetus to live beyond his allotted span, providing he could find a substitute to meet death in his place.

The household god Lars.

LARS

A Roman household god, who shared the hearth along with **Vesta** and Penates, usually portrayed as a happy young man who co-existed easily with the others. He was honored on all the significant and important family occasions, such as weddings, births, and deaths.

LEDA

According to the most familiar tradition, Leda was a daughter of Thestius, king of Aetolia, and married Tyndareus, king of Sparta. However, some of her children were fathered by **Zeus**. These are normally given as **Helen** of Troy and either both the **Dioscuri** (Castor and Pollux), or else just Pollux alone. The parentage of Helen is subject to debate; it was said that she was really the daughter of Zeus and the goddess **Nemesis**. In order to avoid Zeus' advances, Nemesis is said to have changed herself into many different forms, including a goose. Zeus transformed himself into a swan and their embrace provided a favorite Classical and Renaissance artistic sub-

Lars.

ject. Nemesis abandoned the egg that resulted from the union, and it was picked up by a herdsman who took it to Leda. When Helen hatched from it, Leda claimed her for her own on account of the child's great beauty. However, from the time of Euripides onward, it was accepted that Leda gave birth to one egg (or occasionally two) as a result of her own love for Zeus.

The story of the egg is, in all probability, related to a Minoan-Mycenaean tale of deities in bird shape. Although later writers either disbelieved or ridiculed the story, fragments of the enormous shell were preserved at the temple of Leucippidae in Sparta.

LETO

One of the Titans (the first generation of Greek gods), she was the daughter of the Coeus and Phoebe and mother to twin gods, **Apollo** and **Artemis**, whose father was **Zeus**. Knowing that Leto's children would be greater than her own, the jealous **Hera** constrained Leto to travel far and wide in search of a sheltered place where she might bear her divine twins. Finally, the barren island of Ortygia received her and, because the god of light first saw daylight there, changed its name to Delos, the Brilliant. A different legend claimed the birth to have taken place on the island of **Poseidon**, where Zeus created a screen against the sun's rays by forming a wave-shaped arch out of seawater. Leto's birth pains lasted nine days and nine nights on account of the fact that Hera delayed the arrival of Eileithyia (the goddess of childbirth) for some time. Apollo and Artemis later took vengeance on Hera and other persecutors of their mother.

LUCRETIA

While engaged on a siege at Ardrea, Lucretia's husband, Tarquinius Collatinus, and his fellow commanders rode back to Rome to test the loyalty of their wives. One of the commanders, Sextus Tarquinius, was so aroused by Lucretia's beauty that he later burst into her room and raped her. Summoning her husband, father, and other nobles to avenge this crime, she stabbed herself. According to Roman legend, this incident resulted in the insurrection led by Junius Brutus and the expulsion of the Tarquins from Rome. The story is told by Livy and is the subject of Shakespeare's poem *The Rape of Lucrece*.

M

MAAT

Egyptian goddess whose name is frequently translated as "Truth," but who was more universal in that she personified the balanced order established by the sun-god, whose daughter she was, at the time of creation. She was the antithesis of the chaotic forces of "non-existence" that threatened to crash through the sky and destroy the world. Maat's symbol was the ostrich feather. In her name the heiroglyph of a sloping plinth represented the primeval mound. The throne of **Osiris** often rested upon the plinth of Maat, and, in the world of the living in Egypt, the pharaoh derived his authority to govern by upholding the laws of Maat. A crucial scene in Egyptian temple decoration shows the monarch presenting the effigy of Maat, as a seated woman wearing a feather on her head, to the major deity of the sanctuary. In the Hall of Two Truths in the Underworld the goddess was the counterweight to the claims of the heart of the dead person in the scales before the 42 assessor gods.

Maat, goddess of truth and justice.

MARDUK

In the Babylonian creation epic, it was Marduk who conquered Tiamat and saved the gods from destruction, although in Assyrian sources this was attributed to the Assyrian national god, Assur. The gods **Ea** and Anu had failed against Tiamat, so the young Marduk undertook the battle in exchange for recognition as the representative of the gods, with civic and military powers, and also the power over life and death. His successful conquest of Tiamat led to his creation of the cosmos from her body. The gods proclaimed him as their king and leader, and one tablet of the epic is devoted to a learned and laudatory exposition of the 50 names of Marduk. He was annually reinstated as king of the gods in the New Year rites held in the Akitu House when the creation epic was recited.

In the first millennium BC, Marduk was often referred to as Bel, "Lord." The increasing synchronization of Marduk with other important gods of the pantheon is exemplified in a small cuneiform tablet that explains each god as a particular aspect of Marduk himself. **Ninurta**, for instance, is Marduk of the pick, and this has been seen by some scholars as a move toward monotheism. His particular symbols are the pointed triangular spade, found commonly on cylinder seals and boundary stones, and the mythical beast called Mushhushshu. This is a composite leonine monster with a horned snake's head, scaly body and eagle's talons, well-known from the glazed brick representations on the **Ishtar** Gate at Babylon, built by Nebuchadnezzar II.

MARS

Roman god of war and agriculture and the most important god after **Jupiter**, Mars was equated with the Greek god **Ares** and was consequently regarded as the son of **Juno**. The Romans believed that the goddess Juno bore Mars after she had been impregnated by a flower, whereas the Greeks attributed the paternity of Ares to **Zeus**. Mars' fatherhood of **Romulus** by Rhea Silvia, a vestal virgin, founded the Roman race. He had come to Rhea Silvia while she was asleep and she bore him Romulus and **Remus**.

Mars' functions appear to have evolved as the Romans themselves evolved from an agricultural to a warlike nation. Since the month named after him, March (originally the first month of the Roman year), saw both the rebirth of the agricultural year and the start of the campaigning season, the combination of his functions was natural to an agricultural people increasingly engaged in war. Mars had his own priest and altar at Rome, and his sacred animals were the wolf and the woodpecker. A number of festivals were dedicated to him, among them a horse race (14 March) and the purification of sacred trumpets (23 March) originally used in war. His festi-

Mars the Roman god of war.

Venus and Mars.

val in October indicates a time when both soldiers and farmers would lay aside their tools and weapons. Mars' love for **Venus** was early established as a favorite subject for artists.

MARYSAS

A Phrygian satyr of Greek mythology. Having invented the flute, **Athena** put a curse on it and threw it away in disgust when she saw, in a reflection of herself in water, how distorted her cheeks were when playing it. Marysas, on finding the flute, was so captivated by the beauty of its sound that he challenged **Apollo** to make music of equal beauty on his lyre. The first trial resulting in a draw, Apollo challenged Marysas to play his flute upside down. The Muses adjudged Apollo the victor and Marysas was tied to a tree and flayed alive, the blood—or else the tears of his friends, the satyrs—forming the River Marysas. Afterwards, Apollo so regretted his anger that he broke his lyre. The flaying of Marysas was a theme frequently used by classical vase painters and western artists.

MEDEA

"The cunning one" in Greek mythology, daughter of Aeetes, king of the Colchians, and his wife the Oceanid Eidyia, granddaughter of Helios and niece of **Circe**. She is universally said to have been a witch, but is also sometimes seen as a goddess. A much later legend, related by Diodorus, informs us that Medea was a princess of great humanity.

When **Jason** arrived at Colchis with the **Argonauts** in his quest for the Golden Fleece, **Hera**, who wished to punish King Pelias, made Medea fall passionately in love with Jason. She then used her magical powers to assist Jason in his quest, giving him magic ointment that made him impervious to the attacks of fire-breathing bulls, told him how to defeat the soldiers who would spring from the dragon's teeth, and drugged, or killed, the serpent that guarded the Golden Fleece. She also engineered the Argonauts escape from Aeetes. In one version of the story, she murdered and cut into little pieces her younger brother, Apsyrtus, scattering the fragments to delay her father in his pursuit. In other versions, Apsyrtus is grown up and leading the pursuit, until Medea tricks him into a parley where he is treacherously murdered by Jason. Circe later purified the pair of their guilt, but after hearing the grisly details of the crime she also cursed them. Later in their journey, Medea helped Jason kill Talos, the bronze man of Crete. At Iolcos she took vengeance on Pelias, firstly restoring Jason's father, Aeson, to youth by boiling him in a cauldron of magic herbs, and then persuading the daughters of Pelias to do the same, only this time without the magic herbs. In retaliation for the subsequent death of Paellas, his son, Acastrus, drove Jason and Medea into exile. They settled in Corinth and at this point the story diverges markedly. The most famous version, found in the tragedy of Euripedes, has Jason growing tired of Medea and arranging to marry the daughter of Creon, king of Corinth. Medea's anger is aroused and, fearing her vengeance, Creon banishes her and her two children. Coaxing him into a day's delay, Media then kills Creon, his daughter, and her own children by Jason. Finally, taunting Jason in his despair, she escapes to Athens.

MEDUSA

Of the three **Gorgons**, Medusa was the only one who was mortal. Anyone who looked at her was turned to stone. Medusa was hated by **Athena** for making love to **Poseidon** in a temple dedicated to her. She therefore appeared to **Perseus**, presenting him with a bronze shield and instructions on how to kill

Medusa.

Medusa. Using a cap of invisibility, Perseus flew over the oceans and found the Gorgons. Keeping clear of the other two immortal sisters he advanced on Medusa using the shield as a mirror, and then decapitated her with the sword of **Hermes**. He then successfully evaded Medusa's sisters and fled.

MELEAGER

At his birth, the Fates declared that Meleager should continue to live as long as a log that was on the fire was not consumed. His mother, Althaia, preserved this brand. Some time later Meleager's father, Oeneus, king of Calydon, omitted to sacrifice to **Artemis** who, in her anger, sent a huge boar to ravage Calydon. Meleager killed the boar and gave the skin as a trophy to the virgin huntress **Atalanta**, who had been the first to wound it. When his maternal uncles tried to steal the skin from Atalanta, Meleager killed them. Hearing of this, Althaia burned the brand that she had kept, thereby causing the death of her son. The hunt of the Calydonian boar was a favorite subject in Hellenistic art.

MENELAUS

In Greek myth king of Sparta, son of **Atreus**, younger brother of **Agamemnon**, and husband of **Helen**, whom **Paris** carried off to Troy, thus bringing about the Trojan War. Menelaus and Helen lived peacefully in Sparta until Helen was abducted while Menelaus was attending the funeral of his grandfather, Catreus, in Crete. Receiving the news, Menelaus returned to Sparta and gathered around him all those who had unsuccessfully wooed her, for they had all sworn an oath to help the successful suitor should he ever need it. Menelaus took part in a 60-ship expedition under the command of Agamemnon, with the blessing of **Hera**, who hated Paris, her personal enemy.

In the *Iliad*, Menelaus features prominently in the dramatic events at Troy, while the Trojans mocked him for his cowardice, he is portrayed as courageous by Homer. Menelaus agreed to settle the dispute by means of a duel with Paris. He defeated Paris, but was prevented from killing him when **Aphrodite** carried him off on a cloud. Agamemnon pointed out that Menelaus was obviously the victor, and the Trojans hesitated, but Pandarus fired an arrow at Menelaus and grazed him in an attempt to keep the war going. He was successful and the battle resumed, with Menelaus fighting bravely and managing to rescue the body of **Patroclus**.

Menelaus appeared again in the events subsequent to the *Iliad*. Upon Paris' death he had his corpse mutilated. Later Menelaus appears among the warriors inside the Wooden Horse. There are several conflicting accounts of the eventual meeting of Menelaus and his wife Helen, and of **Odysseus**' role in this meeting. In one, a vengeful Menelaus falls in love with her all over again as he is on the point of killing her. After eight years of travelling, they finally returned home to Sparta.

MERCURY

A Roman god, son of Maia and **Jupiter** and introduced at an early date from a Greek or Graeco-Etruscan source. He is closely identified with the Greek god **Hermes**, with the same caduceus (wand), broad-rimmed hat, winged sandals, and purse. Like Hermes, he protected merchants, indeed his name contains the root of the word merx, meaning merchandise.

Mercury, messenger of the gods.

MERETSEGER

In Egyptian mythology, the cobra-goddess dwelling on the peak overlooking the tombs of the pharaohs in the Valley of the Kings. The name Meretseger means "She who loves silence." The official tombworkers, who lived in the village of Deir-el-Medina, regarded Meretseger as a dangerous goddess who could violently react against anyone guilty of perjury or related crimes by poisoning them with her venomous bite.

MIDAS

Midas, the legendary king of Phrygia, having entertained Silenus, the companion of **Dionysus**, was granted a wish. He wished that all he touched might turn to gold, but upon discovering that this also applied to his food, he asked to be relieved of his wish. He was instructed to wash in the River Paetolus which, ever since, has had sands containing gold. A different strand of the myth would have it that Midas was so curious to learn the wisdom of Silenus that he made him drunk by mixing wine with his water. He was then told a parable to the effect that riches do not bring happiness.

MIN

Ancient Egyptian fertility god and the symbol of procreative sexuality. He was shown wearing a tall plumed crown, balancing a flagellum on his fingertips, his phallus proudly announcing his readiness for sexual union. He was the guardian god of nomads and hunters, and his particular domain was the eastern desert. The festival of Min, commemorated in Theban mortuary temples, was a ceremony of the celebration of fecundity in nature and regeneration of life in a way that hinted at the royal jubilee of rejuvenation rituals.

King Midas.

Minerva.

MINERVA

The Roman goddess of crafts and trade, and of the intellectual activity necessary to their successful practice. Minerva was identified with the Greek goddess Pallas **Athena**, and took over her martial characteristics. Together with **Jupiter** and **Juno** she was one of the great Capitoline triad and was introduced to Rome by an Etruscan contingent that came to the aid of **Romulus**. Minerva's festival was the Quinquartus (19 March).

MINOS

Legendary king of Crete, said to have lived three generations before the Trojan War. He was the son of **Europa** and **Zeus**, and was brought up by Asterion, king of Crete, after whose death he became sole ruler, raising up a bull from the sea to prove his right to the succession. Minos' reign was one of justice

Minerva awakes Endymion.

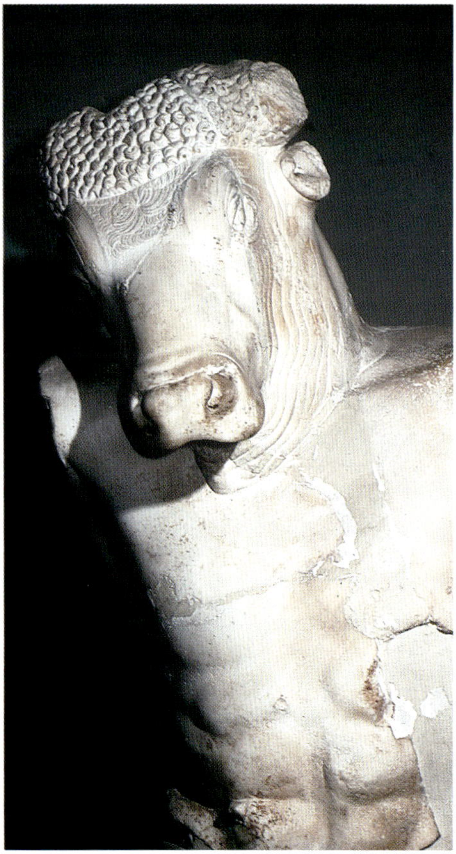
The Minotaur.

and equity. Indeed his laws were considered so remarkable that they were thought to have been directly inspired by Zeus, whom he is said to have consulted every nine years. The portrayal of Minos in Greek myth is in contrast to the Attic legends, which cast him as an evil figure exacting tribute from Athens, as told in the story of **Theseus**. The discrepancy is probably explained by the real contest between Attica and Crete. Having expelled his brother, Rhadamanthys, Minos initiated his legislative ideas. In the Underworld, both Minos and Rhadamanthys sat in judgment over the souls of the dead, assisted by Aecus. Minos was a womanizer, but was also supposed to be the originator of homosexuality. He was killed in his bath by one of the daughters of **Daedalus**, king of Sicily.

MINOTAUR (See THESEUS)
A monster with a bull's head and a man's body, the son of **Pasiphae**, wife of King **Minos** of Crete, and the bull sent by **Poseidon**. Minos had the Athenian

architect **Daedalus**, construct a vast palace (the Labyrinth) comprising such a maze of rooms that only the architect could find his way. Shutting the monster in the labyrinth, Minos fed him seven young men and seven young women, which was the annual tribute exacted from Athens. Theseus volunteered himself to be one of the victims and, with the help of **Ariadne** (the daughter of Minos), not only killed the Minotaur but also found his way out again.

MITHRAS

An ancient Indo-Iranian god whose cult spread via Greece to the Roman world in the second half of the first century BC. The cult of Mithras—whose titles included Lord of Light, Giver of Bliss, and the Victorious—proved attractive particularly to the military and mercantile class. The cult was exclusively confined to men, and involved initiation rites, tests, and ordeals. Mithras was depicted in Roman art as a young warrior wearing the Phrygian cap and Persian trousers. Temples to Mithras were built underground, recalling the cave in which Mithras was alleged to have sacrificed a bull.

MUT

In Egyptian mythology a mother-goddess allied to the pharaoh in her aspect as the consort of **Amun**, the monarch's symbolic father. She was shown as a lithe elegant woman, with a vulture headdress and often wearing the double crown of Upper and Lower Egypt. Her dress was brightly colored and sometimes suggested the feathers of a vulture, a creature sacred to Mut. Her original nature was leonine, from which developed her association with the cat, and many votive statues were dedicated to her in this form.

Mithras.

N

NARCISSUS

A beautiful youth, son of the River Cephissus (in Boetia) and the nymph Liriope. When he was young, his mother asked the seer Tiresias whether he would live long. Tiresias answered enigmatically: "He will if he never knows himself." Narcissus repulsed all lovers, both men and women. Among them was **Echo**, who, deprived of original speech, tried to seduce Narcissus with fragments of his own speech. According to Ovid, Narcissus was punished for his cruelty to Echo when a rejected lover prayed to **Nemesis**, who condemned him to the contemplation of his own beauty in a pool on Mount Helicon. The more he looked the deeper he fell in love, until finally he wasted away and died, and was turned into the narcissus flower.

Neith.

NEITH

In Egyptian myth a creator-goddess with a warlike aspect associated with the western Delta town of Sais. Her ancient emblem was a shield with crossed arrows, and this bellicose aspect comes through her epithet "Lady of the Bow and Ruler of Arrows," which made it easy for the Greeks to identify her with their own goddess **Athena**. The fullest account of Neith's role as a creator-goddess can be found on the columns of Esna temple in Upper Egypt. It was at Esna, according to the legend, that Neith rose up out of the primeval water to create the universe. She was then carried on the Nile flood with the Lates-fish (Esna was called Latopolis or Lates-Fishtown) until she reached the region of Sa-el-Hagar, where she founded Sais. In the Pyramid Age, Neith was stated to be the mother of the crocodile god **Sobek**, but her role as the consort of **Set** was never fully developed, at least not in the sources that have survived.

NEKHBET

Egyptian goddess, protective deity of royalty, possessing an ancient sanctuary on the east bank of the Nile at Nekheb (modern el-Kab). She took the form of a vulture, often with her wings spread and her talons holding symbols of eternity. She symbolized the sway of kingship and, like her northern counterpart **Wadjet**, could appear on the crown of the pharaoh. She even adopted bovine imagery as the "Great White Cow dwelling in Nekheb" to play the role of nurse to the royal children.

NEMESIS

The daughter of Nyx (Night) and the personification of righteous anger, Nemesis is unusual in being both a goddess and an abstract concept. In her divine form she was pursued by **Zeus**, assuming 1000 different forms in order to evade him. Finally she succumbed in the form of a goose when he became a swan. **Helen** of Troy and the **Dioscuri** were born from the resulting egg. In this legend Nemesis personifies divine vengeance. Like the Roman Fors Fortuna, Nemesis was charged with curbing all excessive good fortune or the pride of kings. This reflects a fundamental concept of Greek thought, that any man who rises above his condition exposes himself to divine reprisals. Thus Croesus, who was too wealthy and powerful, was enticed by Nemesis into his expedition against Cyrus, which ruined him. Nemesis was worshipped at Rhammis in Attica, where a magnificent temple was built for her in the fifth century BC.

NEOPTOLEMUS

Also known as the Young Warrior and as Pyrrhus, he was the son of **Achilles** and Deidamia, who was the daughter of Lycomedes, king of Scyros. Neoptolemus was born at a time when Achilles, for his own safety, was living disguised as a girl called Pyrrha in Lycomedes' harem. Neoptolemus was brought up by his grandfather, since Achilles, his father, was engaged in the Trojan War. After his father's death, **Odysseus** was sent as a messenger to summon Neoptolemus to the siege of Troy as a necessary condition for taking the city. Concealing himself in the Trojan Horse, Neoptolemus brutally killed the Trojan king **Priam** and princess Polyxena and carried off Andromache (the widow of **Hector**) and Helenus, a son of Priam, as a prize.

NEPHTHYS

Egyptian goddess whose original prominence, if any, was completely overshadowed by her sister **Isis**. The name of Nephthys means "Mistress of the Mansion/Temple." She had a minimal role as the consort of **Set**, but a liaison with her brother, **Osiris**, led to her giving birth to the jackal-god **Anubis**. Nephthys was a funerary goddess, one of the protectors of the Canopic chest containing the jars of a deceased person's viscera. Her hair tresses seem to symbolize mummy wrappings, and, in the form of a kite, she guarded the dead person's funerary bed in the same way as she assisted Isis to protect the couch on which Osiris lay.

NEPTUNE

The Roman god identified with **Poseidon**. He was the god of water and since the Romans were not in early times a sea-faring people, he was a water-deity of little importance. Indeed he had no legend specific to himself until his assimilation with the Greek god Poseidon. In Roman tradition, Neptune was said to have a companion spirit called Amphitrite, Salacia, or Venilia. His festival was celebrated at the height of the summer (23 July), during the driest season

Roman god of the sea Neptune.

NERGAL
An important Mesopotamian god, chiefly associated with death and the Underworld, with whom several originally separate gods such as Meslamatae'a or Lugalgirra, and most especially Erra, were identified. He was the son of **Enlil** and Ninlil, and in some texts he is a bellicose warrior rather similar to **Ninurta**. His cult city was Kutha in southern Iraq, where he was worshipped with his consort Laz in his temple Emeslam. As ruler of the realm of the dead, his wife was Ereshkigal, and the "Myth of Nergal and Ereshkigal", of which copies have been found at El Amarna in Egypt and Sultantepe in Turkey, explain the circumstances under which Nergal came to rule there. Erra was a violent deity responsible for inflicting plague on mankind, and he features prominently in the *Erra Epic*. Here Erra, briefly in control of cosmic matters in the absence of **Marduk**, lays Babylon waste with disastrous results, which have been taken to reflect historical troubles caused by the incursion of nomads into the Mesopotamian heartland.

NIKE
The ancient Greek goddess of victory, daughter of the river nymph Styx and the Titan Pallas. Nike was honored by **Zeus** for taking the part of the gods in the war against the Titans. From this she became the manifestation of earthly victory, with athletes, charioteers, soldiers, and politicians praying to her for success.

NINHURSAG
"Lady of the Mountain," one of the Mesopotamian mother-goddesses, described in Sumerian as "Mother of the Gods," and "Mother of All Children," and addressed as mother by many early rulers in their royal inscriptions. Other mother-goddesses are mentioned in mythological and literary texts, of whom Ninmah, Nintu, Mama/Mami, and Beletili are perhaps the best known. Ninhursag's symbol is the uterus.

NINURTA
"Lord of the Earth," an important Sumero-Babylonian god, the son of **Enlil**, worshipped especially in the city of Nippur in the temple Eshumesha. His wife is given as Gula, the goddess of healing, and his identity is often blended with that of the god Ningirsu, sometimes also as Bau, the latter's wife. His exploits feature prominently in two lengthy bilingual (Sumerian and Akkadian) poems. The first, *King Storm whose fearfulness is Frightful*, celebrates his defeat of the mythical monster Asag, located in the mountainous areas to the east of Mesopotamia, using stones to control the water supplies for the Tigris and the Euphrates rivers. It is considered to be a nature myth primarily concerned with the age-old preoccupation with rainfall and irrigation. The second, *Fashioned like An*, describes Ninurta's triumphant return to his city, Nippur. His character is multi-faceted: originally perhaps a god of the plough, venerated by farmers, it is Ninurta who imparts agricultural knowledge in a technical composition sometimes termed the Sumerian Georgica. His alter ego was the storm/thunder-god called **Anzu**, who was once defeated by Ninurta according to a fragmentary myth. His prowess as a warrior is celebrated in many texts, and particularly by the later Assyrian kings. Ninurta had an important temple at Nimrud, and appears to be shown in surviving carved scenes from its walls. His symbol is the plough.

Nike, goddess of Victory.

NIOBE

The name of two quite separate classical heroines. One was the daughter of the first man, Phoroneus, by the nymph Teledice. She was **Zeus**' first human mistress and bore him Argus. The other and better known was the daughter of the Lydian king **Tantalus** and of Dione; she married Amphione of Thebes, by whom she had seven daughters. On the feast day of **Leto** at Thebes, she expressed scorn for Leto who had produced only two offspring, **Apollo** and **Aretemis**. Affronted, Leto called on her children to avenge the slight. The twin gods responded and punished Niobe's arrogance by striking down her children with fatal arrows. She was left with one son and one daughter, and, overcome with grief, she regretted her affront to Leto. In their pity the gods turned her into a rock from which flowed a spring of tears.

NUMA-POMPILIUS

The mythical second king of Rome, who, according to tradition, reigned from 715–673 BC. He was born on the same day that **Romulus** founded Rome and, on account of his piety, was invited to succeed him. He was credited with founding most of the cults and sacred institutions of Rome. His religious policy was inspired by the nymph Egeria who came at night to give him advice in the grotto of the Camenae near a sacred spring. The institution of a calendar based on the phases of the moon, and the distinction between *dies fasti* and *dies refrasti* were attributed to him, along with many other cultural attributions. Numa possessed magic powers, such as the ability to create sumptuous dishes from nothing, and was given credit for persuading **Jupiter** to content himself with turning thunder aside with onion heads, instead of the heads of men. He died at an extremely great age and was buried on the right of the River Tiber on the Janiculum.

NUN

In Egyptian mythology the personification of primeval watery chaos. His title of "Father of the Gods" refers to this original existence as the substance out of which creation began. However once **Atum** emerged spontaneously out of Nun to create the cosmos, Nun had no further role to play. The concept of Nun as the primeval matter is preserved in temple complexes, where a sacred lake served both to symbolize Nun and to provide a service for ritual ablutions.

NUT

An Egyptian cosmic goddess representing the vault of the sky, daughter of the air-god **Shu** and moisture-goddess **Tefnut**. Her consort is her brother, the earth-god **Geb**, above whose prone body she arches her own, her hands and feet at the four cardinal points. Although depicted as separated from Geb by the air-god Shu, her sexual union with him produced the four children who form the link between the cosmic deities and the throne of Egypt: **Osiris**, **Isis**, **Set**, and **Nephthys**. In the tomb of Seti I (1306–1290 BC) in the Valley of the Kings, Nut is shown as the great celestial cow with the sun-god sailing across the underside of her body. The strength of Nut prevented the ungovernable forces of chaos from devastating the Two Lands. Her relationship with the sun-god is a fascinating contradiction. In the theogony of Heliopolis she is the granddaughter of the sun-god **Re**, but one explanation of his nightly disappearance was that Nut swallowed him to give birth to the sun again at dawn.

O

ODYSSEUS

The most famous hero of all classical antiquity. The Latin form is Ulysses. He was the son of Laertes, king of Ithaca, and Anticlea. Odysseus was one of the suitors for the hand of **Helen**, and so when she was carried off to Troy he was bound (as were all the other suitors) to help rescue her. Although he feigned madness to escape obligations to Helen's father (ironic as he was the originator of that oath), he is subsequently portrayed in the *Iliad* as not only cunning and energetic but also as good in counsel as in battle.

Odysseus played an important part in many of the key events of the Trojan War, particularly in missions involving either diplomacy, oratory, or espionage. Thus it was he who was placed in charge of the mission to **Achilles** when **Agamemnon** sought a reconciliation with the latter. Odysseus is also credited with the idea of the Wooden Horse, and was the first to leap out of it, when he accompanied **Menelaus** on his quest for Helen. After the death of Achilles, a quarrel arose between **Ajax**, son of Telamon, and Odysseus in the contest for the dead man's armor. The power of his oratory persuaded the army that he was the most deserving of this honor since it was he who had served the Greeks best.

Odysseus hears the sirens while strapped to the mast of his ship.

Later, on his way home from Troy, Odysseus was held prisoner by the Cyclops, a one-eyed giant, but he was able to escape under the belly of a ram when the Cyclops became drunk on the wine he had brought as a token of friendship. Odysseus then reached the island of Aeolus, the Warden of the Winds, where he was given a bag containing all the winds except the one necessary to blow him back to Ithaca. He and his companions were within sight of their homeland when Odysseus fell asleep, and one of the companions opened the bag, freeing all the winds, which blew them back to King Aeolus again. After many more adventures, including a shipwreck in which all the others died, Odysseus returned to

Ithaca, showered with gifts from Alcinous, some 20 years since his departure for Troy.

Penelope, Odysseus' wife, was waiting for him, resisting the demands of 108 suitors by saying that she would give one of them an answer once she had finished weaving a shroud for old Laertes. This she wove by day and unpicked by night. Odysseus returned to the palace dressed as a beggar and, although he spoke to his wife, he withheld his identity from her. For her part, she had arranged an archery competition between the suitors the next day, the winner of which would win her hand. The competitors would use Odysseus' own bow. When it transpired that not one of the 108 could bend it, Odysseus was handed the bow. He accomplished the task at the first shot, going on to kill all the suitors. Odysseus then at last revealed himself to Penelope. The next day he presented himself to his father and then went on to appease his last enemy, the god **Poseidon**, by founding a shrine in his honor.

OEDIPUS

The hero of one of the best known legends in Greek literature, given to us by Sophocles, Aeschylus, and Euripides. Laius, king of Thebes, was warned by an oracle that if he ever had a son, that son would not only kill him but also bring a terrible succession of misfortunes upon his house. To avert this, when Laius fathered Oedipus by Jocasta, he had the boy left on a hillside exposed to the elements, intending his death. To assist this plan, he had Oedipus' ankles pierced so as to join them together with a strap. The boy was found by Corinthian shepherds,

Oedipus solves the riddle of the Theban Sphinx.

Oedipus and the Sphinx.

however, who took him home to their king, Polybus, whom they knew to be childless and in need of an heir. Oedipus was brought up at the court of Polybus until one day it was revealed to him that he was in reality only the adopted son of Polybus. He then set off to consult the Delphic oracle as to the true identity of his parents. On his way there he was insulted by Polphontes, the herald of King Laius. In his anger he slew both the herald and his own father. Frightened by what he had done, Oedipus proceeded to Thebes, where he met the **Sphinx** and successfully guessed her riddle. In doing so not only did he bring about the death of the Sphinx, but also freed the Thebans from its curse. In their gratitude they gave him the hand of their king's widow (his mother), and made him king.

Soon, however, the secret of his birth came to be revealed. In early versions of the story this is because of the scars on his ankles inflicted by his father. A plague then ravaged Thebes and would not cease until Laius' death had been avenged. Oedipus pronounced a curse on the murderer, asking Tiresias the identity of the guilty man. Tiresias dared not answer, bringing suspicion on himself; but Oedipus was seized by a terrible suspicion, which was confirmed when messengers from Corinth informed him that Polybus was dead and that he should go to Corinth, marry the queen and take the throne. This would not be incestuous, they said, because he was a foundling. The account given of the finding of the child left no room for doubt—Oedipus had killed his own father and committed incest with Jocasta. She fled into the palace and killed herself, and Oedipus then blinded himself, falling victim to his own curse. He died in the village of Colonus after long and painful travels.

ONURIS

Egyptian bearded spear-carrying god with a crown of four plumes. A warrior and a hunter, whose most important sanctuary was near Abydos at the ancient city of This. The etymology of his name means "He who Brings Back the Far-off One." In order to gain a consort, Onuris pursued Mekhit, a lioness-goddess, into Nubia, captured her and brought her back to Egypt. His prowess as a hunter gave him the reputation of slaughterer of the enemies of the sun-god.

ORESTES

A son of **Agamemnon** and **Clytemnestra**. Mentioned only briefly by Homer and Hesiod, he was the last major figure of Greek tragedy, his story being told by Aeschylus, Sophocles, and Euripides. The myth has many different versions, but all agree that Orestes was motivated by the desire to avenge the death of his father, Agamemnon, against his mother and her lover Aegisthus. Orestes himself was threatened by his mother's dagger when his sister, **Electra**, spirited him away to be brought up by an uncle.

When he reached manhood, **Apollo** ordered him to avenge his father and kill his mother and her lover. To achieve this he disguised himself as a traveler bearing news of his own death. Thinking herself free from retribution Clytemnestra sent for Aegisthus, whereupon Orestes killed them both. However, despite divine sanction he was then tormented by the **Furies**, and was driven mad. He was tried at Athens and acquitted, but could not recover his sanity until he had stolen the wooden

The head of Orpheus.

statue of **Artemis**, in the land of the stranger-eating Taurians. Fortunately for him, his sister **Iphigenia** turned out to be the priestess of the shrine, and they both escaped with the statue. Orestes went on to become the most powerful monarch in the Peloponnese.

ORPHEUS

The myth of Orpheus is one of the most obscure and symbolic in Greek mythology. Indeed the myth had a certain influence on early Christian belief and iconography. While it is generally accepted that his father was Oeagrus, his mother is more problematical. She is usually given as Calliope, chief of the nine Muses. There are three main legends concerning Orpheus. These are his role on the voyage of the **Argonauts**, his descent into the Underworld and the circumstances surrounding his own death.

His role in the Argosy was important, for, although weaker than the other heroes, he used his voice to great effect. Thus, he stilled the waves during a storm and later saved the Argonauts from the **Sirens** seduction, singing with an even greater sweetness than they.

The descent of Orpheus into the Underworld was a theme developed mainly in the Alexandrian period. Orpheus' wife, **Eurydice**, was pursued by Aristeus. As she fled she was fatally bitten by a serpent. Inconsolable at her tragic death, Orpheus went down into the Underworld to find her. With music from his lyre he charmed all the Underworld guards and gods. **Hades** and **Persephone** agreed to restore Eurydice to him on one condition: that he would not look back at her until he had reached the world outside. Orpheus almost achieved this when, for some reason, he looked back. Immediately Eurydice became a shadow and though he tried to follow her this time he could not pass. Only the sound of his lyre in grottoes or mountains could soothe his grief.

The death of Orpheus has given rise to a number of traditions. In most legends he is killed by the Ciconian women of Thrace, for any one of a number of reasons. After his death the Muses buried him except for his head and his lyre, which were buried in Lesbos. The lyre later rose to the sky as the constellation Lyra.

OSIRIS

The Egyptian god of death and resurrection, and king of the Underworld. Osiris was the eldest offspring of **Geb** and **Nut**, who inherited the throne of Egypt. He introduced agriculture and began civilizing the people. His reign with his sister-wife **Isis** was brought to sudden end in a murderous assault by his brother **Set**. Isis, however, found his body and used her magic powers to prevent decomposition. The god **Thoth** helped embalm him and **Anubis** presided over the ritual. Through her magic, Isis was also able to impregnate herself from Osiris, with their son to be, **Horus**, who would ultimately topple Set and assume his inheritance. Osiris then vanished from the stage of Egypt to become the ruler of the Underworld. Although originally linked exclusively to royalty, with time Osiris became more democratic, until anyone who had lived a true life and successfully passed the Judgment of **Maat** could join him in the afterlife.

Osiris, god of the Egyptian Underworld.

P, Q

PAN

Greek god of flocks and shepherds, worshipped widely in Greece after the fifth century BC. He lived in Arcadia in a grotto, spending his time chasing nymphs and dancing. Renowned for his sexual energy, he was goat-like in appearance, though he stood on his hind legs. He instructed **Apollo** in prophecy and invented the syrinx or panpipes. In Roman times he was identified with the woodland god Faunus.

The earth god Pan.

PANDORA

The first woman on earth, she plays an important part in numerous versions of the Greek creation myth. Her name means "all gifts" and reflects her story. When **Prometheus** stole fire for mankind, a furious **Zeus** ordered **Hephaestus** to make a woman out of earth who, with her charm and beauty, would bring misery to all humans, and she did! When Prometheus' brother, Epimetheus, saw her, he instantly forgot his brother's warning to reject gifts from Zeus, and thus began man's misery.

The story of Pandora's "box" gives a further explanation of human misery. Curious as to the content of a large earthenware pot, Pandora lifted the lid. Alas, it was Epimetheus' pot, containing all the evils of the world and just one good, namely **Hope**. The evils escaped when the lid was removed, leaving just Hope at the bottom.

PARIS

The son of **Priam** in Greek legend, Paris was originally exposed at birth by his mother, Hecuba, following a nightmare prophecy. He was brought up by shepherds on Mount Ida, but his identity was eventually revealed when he won all the events at his own Trojan funeral games and was recognized by his sister **Cassandra**.

Pandora carried to Olympus by Vulcan.

Paris, prince of Troy.

It was while living on Mount Ida that Paris was drawn into the fateful beauty contest between **Hera**, **Athena**, and **Aphrodite**. Nobody wanted to be the judge, and so Paris was selected to make the decision. Hera promised to make him ruler of all Asia, Athena offered him wisdom and victory, but he chose Aphrodite who said she would give him the love of the most beautiful woman in the world—**Helen** of Sparta. Thus was set in train the events of the Trojan War, so central to the whole of Greek mythology.

PASIPHAE

In Greek myth the wife of **Minos**, king of Crete, mother of **Ariadne** and the **Minotaur**. She was the sister of **Circe** and shared some of her ability in sorcery. When **Poseidon** sent the white bull from the sea in answer to Minos' plea for validation of his claim to the throne, he

Achilles binds the wounds of Patroclus.

also caused Pasiphae to develop a passion for it, perhaps to punish her for despising the cult of **Aphrodite**. Consumed with desire, she had **Daedalus** create a lifelike heifer, which she could get inside. In this way, she seduced the bull and then gave birth to the half-man, half-bull Minotaur. She herself was jealous of her husband's love affairs, and put a spell on him that caused any woman to whom he made love to be consumed by serpents coming out of his body.

PATROCLUS

The companion of **Achilles**, who was brought up with him at Phthia. He went to Troy with him, too, ending up taking a crucial part in the fighting. He withdrew from the battle when Achilles withdrew, but then borrowed his friend's armor to fight. He killed many Trojans, but was eventually killed himself by **Hector**. This was the cause of Achilles return to the fray to avenge his death. The body of Patroclus was burnt and the ashes interred in a mound where Achilles too was eventually buried.

PEGASUS

The winged horse of the Greek gods and the Muses, born from the head of **Medusa** when it was severed by **Perseus**, or, in another version, fathered on her by **Poseidon**. Pegasus went to Olympus and carried thunder and lightning for **Zeus**.

The winged horse Pegasus.

He was caught by **Bellerophon** with a special golden bridle, but when Bellerophon became too proud of his conquest of the Chimaera and the Amazons and tried to ride up to heaven, Pegasus, stung by a fly sent from Zeus, threw him off. The beautiful Pegasus eventually became a constellation.

PENELOPE

The faithful wife of **Odysseus**, by whom she had one son, Telemachus. Her husband was reluctant to go to Troy, because he did not want to leave her. During his 20-year absence she had to endure the wooing of over 100 suitors, whom she delayed and deceived by a variety of methods. Finally on Odysseus' return, she recognized him by his strength—he was the only one who could bend his own huge bow, left in the palace. After Odysseus' death, she married Telegonus.

PERSEPHONE **(See HADES)**

Daughter of **Demeter** and **Zeus**, who was worshipped with her mother as goddess of vegetation and growth. The story of her abduction represents an attempt to explain how nature lies dormant for part of the year and then springs forth and restores to life. When Hades kidnapped her, Demeter blamed the land for swallowing her daughter, with winter the consequence, but she was persuaded to seek Zeus' help. The condition that Persephone had eaten nothing underground was broken, and so a compromise was struck: she would spend half her time with Hades and half her time up on earth with Demeter in an explanation of the seasons. This story was taken over by the Romans and assimilated into their goddess Prosperina.

PERSEUS

Mythic Greek hero from Argos, the son of **Zeus** and **Danae**, famed for decapitating the **Gorgon Medusa**. His grandfather, Acrisius, was afraid of a prophecy that if his daughter bore a son, this son would kill him; so, when Danae gave birth, he set mother and son adrift on the sea in a box. They came ashore on the island of Seriphos, where the ruler Polydectes fell in love with Danae and finding that Perseus guarded his mother so well, sent him to destroy Medusa. With the aid of **Hera**, **Hermes**, and the Muses, and their various gifts of special equipment: a shield to act as a mirror, winged sandals to fly, and **Hades**' helmet of invisibility, Perseus easily escaped being turned to stone and won the head of the Gorgon. From her neck sprung the giant Chrysaor and the winged horse **Pegasus**.

On his way home with the head he fell in love with **Andromeda**, who had been chained to a rock as a sacrifice to a sea monster. Perseus used Medusa's head to turn the monster to stone, and then married Andromeda. Returning to Seriphos, he found that Polydectes had tried to rape Danae, and turned him to stone as well. **Athena** took the head and put it in the middle of her shield.

Perseus wanted to see his grandfather again so he returned to Argos, but Acrisius was still afraid of the oracle and fled. The two were both present at a funeral games in Pelasgia, however, where Perseus accidentally killed his grandfather with a discus. This terrible fulfillment of the prophecy left Perseus unable to claim his grandfather's kingdom, so he swapped with his cousin Megapenthes, who became king of Argos, and he himself became king of Tiryns.

Perseus, with the head of the Gorgon Medusa.

The cyclops Polyphemus, being blinded by Odysseus and his crew.

PLUTO

The name used in both Greek and Roman mythology to describe **Hades**, the god-king of the Underworld. The name Pluto means "the rich"—a reference to the plentiful mineral resources beneath the ground and the rich earth above it. In art, he is shown with a cornucopia (a horn of plenty), but he is rarely mentioned in myths, perhaps because it was thought to be bad luck to say his name. There was a temple dedicated to him at Byzantium.

POLYPHEMUS

In Greek myth a Cyclops (one-eyed giant) and son of **Poseidon**, Polyphemus reared sheep and goats, probably in Sicily. In one story he became the lover of the beautiful nymph called Galatea, but was jilted for being too boorish. In the *Odyssey*, Polyphemus finds **Odysseus** and his men hiding in his cave and eats some of them. Still stuck there come evening, Odysseus gets the Cyclops drunk and then blinds him with a stake, completing their narrow escape by narrowly avoiding the rocks hurled by the irate giant.

POSEIDON

One of the Olympian deities of the Greeks, a son of **Cronus** and Rhea. His sphere of power covered the sea, water (not rivers), and earthquakes. He had powers over **Zeus** in these fields, but was ultimately less powerful than his brother. His consort was Amphitrite but he had affairs with **Medusa** and **Demeter**.

Poseidon played an in important part in the Trojan War. He built the walls of Troy with **Apollo**, but on being cheated of his pay sent a sea-monster to scourge the land. This ill-disposed him toward the Trojans, and he actively helped the Greeks, taking on the appearance of Calchas to encourage them. His partici-pation was curtailed by Zeus, but he saved **Aeneas** when **Achilles** was just about to kill him.

PRIAM

King of Troy in the time of the war, Priam was the youngest son of Laomedon. In his youth he had fought the Amazons, but by the time of the Trojan War he was too old to fight, so he presided over councils and was widely respected, even by his enemies and most of the gods, for his wisdom. It was his youngest son, **Paris**, who began it all, and Priam countenanced the abduction of **Helen** by receiving them at Troy. His sadness and desperation at seeing his sons die one by one is well illustrated in Book 24 of the *Iliad*. His wife, Hecuba, stood by him throughout the war, but when at the end he tried to take up arms she persuaded him to take refuge at the altar of **Zeus**. This led to his death, as he first of all had to watch another son, Polites, die at the hand of **Neoptolemus**, the son of **Achilles**, who then also slew him. Although his death was mourned by Hecuba, his body remained unburied.

PRIAPUS

Greek god of fertility, born with a massively enlarged phallus, which was the symbol with which he could ward off the evil eye—statues of him were, therefore, used in gardens to act as scarecrows. He was the son of **Aphrodite**, but **Hera**, jealous of her rival's beauty, made Priapus deformed at birth, and his mother abandoned him. In some stories Priapus is the son of **Dionysus** and certainly their cults were similar.

PROMETHEUS

A Greek demi-god, one of the race of Titans. He created man from clay and so was seen as a master craftsman. He used his natural wiles to steal fire from Olympus, where **Zeus** had hidden it. Having brought the fire to earth inside a smoldering fennel stalk, he duped Zeus again when he was faced with a choice of sacrificial offerings: he chose the larger portion containing all the fat and bones, leaving the smaller, but more valuable, portion for men. Punishment for these tricks came when Zeus brought misery to mankind in the shape of

The long suffering Prometheus.

Prometheus creates the first man.

Pandora, and chained Prometheus to a rock with an eagle sent each day to peck out his liver, which, being immortal, grew back to its full size each night. **Heracles** eventually freed Prometheus, who gained immortality from **Chiron**, who wished to lose his and die. Prometheus was also known for his prophetic powers, and his son, **Deucalion** was warned by him of the imminent flood.

PSYCHE

Means "soul" in Greek. From the earliest times, it was accepted that the soul was separate from the body as its "double." Later, the soul was considered to be a winged spirit that departed from the body at death. All such winged souls were female, and from the fifth century onward were shown as butterflies. The story of Psyche served to elaborate the theory.

Psyche was a most beautiful princess with no suitors, as everyone feared her beauty. Her father, on consulting an oracle, was told to dress her up for marriage and leave her on a rock. This was done, and the girl was wafted away on the wind. On waking she found herself in valley near a large palace, where voices guided her inside and stayed with her in the day, while she had the company of her monster husband each night. She never saw him; if she did, she was told she would lose him forever. Psyche however, on being teased by her sisters that she had never seen her husband, resolved to look. She discovered that he was a most handsome youth, namely Love (**Eros**, **Cupid**) himself, who awoke and fled. Left alone the beautiful Psyche wandered the earth, attracting the jealous attention of **Aphrodite**, who imprisoned her and set her menial tasks. Her last task for Aphrodite was to go down into the Underworld to fetch a flask of the water of youth, but on her way back she opened it and fell into a deep sleep. While she was asleep, Eros found and woke her, asking permission to wed. **Zeus** agreed, and Aphrodite was at last reconciled to her rival.

PTAH

Egyptian creator-god of Memphis, the political and administrative capital of Egypt following unification of the Two Lands around 3000 BC. He is represented anthropomorphically in a tight-fitting linen wrap. A basalt slab, known as the Shabaka Stone, shows Ptah creating the cosmos in a purely metaphysical way. This represents the earliest example of the "logos" doctrine yet discovered. The self-created god conceived the idea of the universe and spoke it into existence through his tongue. This account of the creation of the world ranks as one of the greatest achievements of the Ancient World. Ptah's temple at Memphis, of which almost nothing remains today, was once one of the most impressive in Egypt. He was worshipped there with his consort, the lioness-goddess **Sakhmet**.

Ptah, Lord of Memphis.

R

RE

Egyptian sun-god of Heliopolis, the supreme transcendental deity manifest in the three spheres of the Sky, Earth, and Underworld. Re is really the power of the sun, represented anthropomorphically with a falcon's head wearing a sun disk crown encircled by the protective cobra-goddess. In some myths Re is seen as an aging monarch of the universe, with hair of lapis lazuli, bones of silver, and flesh of gold. The pharaohs of Egypt formulated a way of enhancing their divinity by forging a link with the sun-god, through their pyramids, which symbolized gigantic stairways to the sky (the Egyptian for pyramid was *mer* or "place of ascension") or the rays of the sun.

Romulus and Remus, suckled by the she-wolf.

Re as a creator-god could be visualized as emerging out of the primeval water within a primordial lotus flower, which opened to reveal the newly born god. The tears of the sun-god fell to earth and from them sprung the human race, described in most elevated texts as "the cattle of Re." At night the sun-god, depicted now as ram-headed, traveled in his night boat through the Underworld, bringing light and life to the gods and goddesses there, to emerge transformed once again into the dawn sky.

REMUS

Son of **Rhea Silvia** and **Zeus**, and twin-brother of **Romulus**, the mythical founder of Rome. Remus scorned his brother's attempts at making a preliminary boundary for the new city, and was killed by Romulus for this. His legend probably dates from the fourth century BC.

RENENUTET

Egyptian cobra-goddess, not frequently represented in iconography, but important as a protector of royalty. She appears as a woman with a cobra's head, sometimes suckling a child. Her snake-gaze overcomes all the pharaoh's enemies, and her power was harnessed to the idea of ripening the barley harvest. As "Lady of the Threshing Floor" she kept predators away from the grain in her form of the dangerous cobra. Renenutet also symbolized the magical power in the linen garments worn by the pharaoh, and came to be associated with the linen used in embalming mummified corpses for the afterlife.

RHEA SILVIA

Also known as Ilia, she was the daughter Numitor, the rightful king of Rome. Rhea Silvia was a vestal virgin, and was therefore prevented from marrying. She was secretly loved by **Mars**, however, and had twins by him: **Romulus** and **Remus**. Amulius, who had usurped the throne from his brother, imprisoned her when he realized she was pregnant, but she escaped, dying in childbirth or killed after she had given birth. In another tradition she is the daughter of **Aeneas**.

ROMULUS

Mythical founder of Rome, son of **Mars** and **Rhea Silvia**. The main thread of this much-varied story has Romulus and his brother **Remus** thrown into the River Tiber, then washed ashore and suckled by a she-wolf. They were brought up by a royal herdsman, but were eventually recognized. They then overthrew the king of Alba and decided to found a city of their own nearby. The traditional date for the foundation is 754 BC. Romulus and Remus built their city on the Palatine Hill, but Remus kicked down a new wall, for which act Romulus killed him.

Romulus planned the Rape of the Sabines in order to provide wives for his Romans. During ceremonial games in Rome, to which the Sabines had been invited, the Romans carried off the Sabine women. This led to war, during which the Sabines besieged the Capitol, but the two sides were eventually reconciled. Romulus then disappeared in a thunderstorm, and became the god Quirinius.

The name Rome is taken from Romulus' name, which itself means Roman. The transferring of names betrays the Greek influence of this myth. Romulus represents the Roman people, and his story is the creation story of Rome itself.

S

SAKHMET

Egyptian lioness-goddess of Memphis, very familiar in her form of a graceful female body with a leonine head. Her name meant "Powerful One," which admirably suited her ferocious nature. The sun disk which she wore emphasized her parentage as a daughter of the sun-god **Re**. There is one particular myth attesting to her bloodthirsty character. Re was suspicious that men were plotting to overthrow his rule, and sent his avenging "Eye" down to Egypt. This "Eye of Re" began as **Hathor** but transformed into **Sakhmet** for the slaughter. Sakhmet sought out and killed men, drinking their blood. At night the sun-god wanted to stop the massacre, as no people meant no offerings or upkeep of the temples. He therefore swamped the land with beer disguised as blood, and when Sakhmet resumed killing in the morning she drank the bogus blood and became drunk, forgetting her plan to destroy the final humans. The Egyptians portrayed her as able not only to bring epidemics but also to ward them off. At Memphis, Sakhmet was the consort of **Ptah** and mother of the divine child of their triad, the lotus-god Nefertum.

The leonine Sakhmet.

SARAPIS

A composite god of the Ptolemaic period, created around 300 BC from existing Egyptian and Greek deities, to symbolize the synthesis of the two cultures that the new Greek rulers of Egypt hoped would occur. The concept of this hybrid god was entirely evolved at the court of Alexandria, where the Sarapeum was regarded as one of the Seven Wonders of the Ancient World, drawing pilgrims from far and wide in search of miraculous cures from Sarapis in his aspect of healer.

The name Sarapis was formed from the description of **Apis**, the sacred bull of Memphis after its death as Osiris-Apis or Osorapis. The underlying concept of resurrection combined with the vigor and fertility of the bull.

The iconography of Sarapis is totally Hellenistic, representing the god as a bearded man with the symbol of agricultural prosperity on his head.

SARGON OF AKKAD

Historical ruler and founder of the Semitic Old Akkadian dynasty, who united the cities of Mesopotamia into an effective empire for the first time. Sargon is the subject of a cycle of stories and traditions, but also occurs in a myth called the "Sargon Legend." This narrates how Sargon, ignorant of his father's identity, was born in secret to a high priestess, who placed him in a reed basket sealed with pitch, which she then deposited in the river. A water-drawer called Aqqi rescued the boy and brought him up, teaching him to be a gardener. The boy later became king. This theme, the so-called "infant exposure" motif, has echoes in other literatures of the ancient world, notably that of Moses from the Bible.

SATURN

An ancient Italian god, identified with the Greek **Cronus** and Near Eastern **Baal**, he also had all the attributes of **Demeter**. The worship of Saturn focused strongly on the Saturnalia, or festival of Saturn, held each year at the end of December. This was a happy celebration involving role-reversal, where masters took orders from their slaves. From about the fourth century these celebrations became assimilated into those of New Year's Day and Christmas. The temple of Saturn, on the Capitoline Hill, was used as a treasury.

Saturn was the god who civilized Italy, teaching cultivation, following on from **Janus**. With agriculture central to wealth-creation, it was natural for him to be regarded as a god of plenty. He ruled over a golden age and then suddenly disappeared, in the way of mythical kings.

SELKET

Selket was a protective scorpion-goddess and a daughter of the ancient Egyptian sun-god **Re**. She watched over the sky with **Neith**, to prevent anyone interrupting Amun and his wife, and so was also a guardian-goddess of conjugal union. Selket was represented as a woman with a scorpion's head or a scorpion with a woman's head, as well as a complete woman. In her funerary aspect she was the assistant and guard of Qebehesenuef, the custodian of the viscera. She also helped the deceased orient themselves in the Underworld, and was believed to bind **Apophis**, the gigantic evil serpent who was a manifestation of darkness and death. In the world of the living, she was a kind of patron-saint for healers and magicians, and a protective deity against venomous bites and poison.

SEMELE

Daughter of **Cadmus**, king of Boetian Thebes, and the mother, by **Zeus**, of the god **Dionysus**. Her affair with Zeus was interrupted by the jealousy of **Hera**, who persuaded her to test her lover's divinity by asking him to appear in his true shape. He appeared as a thunderbolt (his true shape), and Semele was struck dead; but her newly-conceived son was made immortal by the thunderbolt. Zeus lodged Dionysus in his thigh until he was born. When he was old enough, Dionysus went down into the Underworld to fetch Semele and took her back up to Olympus to be a goddess. Semele was also loved by **Actaeon**, who was punished for rivaling Zeus.

The beautiful scorpion goddess Selket.

SET

Egyptian god of great antiquity and power whose nature incorporated elemental forces of chaos. Set was one of the children of **Nut** and **Geb** in the Heliopolitan Ennead, but was certainly a god of entirely independent origin, with strong support in the north-east Delta and in Upper Egypt around his birthplace of Ombos. Set also had adherents in the royal families of various dynasties. He could also readily equate, as a god of storms and battle, with Middle Eastern gods such as **Baal**, or the Hittite storm-god **Teshub**. In addition, the goddesses **Ishtar** and Anat entered the Egyptian pantheon as wives of Set.

In the legend of **Osiris** from the Pyramid age onward, Set was regarded as a murderer and usurper of the throne. (His popularity was not helped by being chosen as the chief deity of an occupying foreign dynasty known as the Hyksos.) Although Set lost the contest for the throne, his strongest ally remained the sun-god **Re**, who took him on board his solar bark as a vital crew-member.

SHAMASH

The Mesopotamian sun-god and god of justice and fair play, responsible for communication by omen, Shamash equates with the Sumerian god Utu. Regarded as the son of the moon-god, **Sin**, and brother of **Ishtar**, Shamash is possessed of a consistently benevolent character in the sources. Mythologically, he was conceived in Mesopotamian thought to cross over the heavens in the day, traversing the Underworld by night. A famous cylinder seal shows Shamash emerging in the morning, with his characteristic symbol of a saw. According to the *Epic of **Gilgamesh***, this took place at Mount

The deadly Set.

Mashum. While in the Underworld, Shamash was considered responsible for the spirits of the dead, and he plays an important role in magic against ghosts and witches. His symbol was a four-pointed star with wavy lines, in a circle.

SHU
Originally an Egyptian solar divinity, who became subordinated to the idea of air or sunlight separating his two off-spring—the sky-goddess **Nut** and the earth-god **Geb**—by physically supporting the sky with his arms or by sailing between the two in a boat. A reference to the "Bones of Shu" probably describe the clouds in the sky.

SILVANUS
Roman god of the woods, gardens, and forests, Silvanus was the son of a shepherd and a goat. He was portrayed as a satyr, with the body of a man and the legs of a goat. Like Faunus he is seen as the Roman equivalent of the Greek god **Pan**.

SIN
The Mesopotamian moon god, who equates to the Sumerian Nanna-Su'en, Sin was the son of **Enlil** and Ninlil, husband of Ningal, and father to **Shamash** and **Ishtar**. His principal cult was located in the ancient city of Ur.

SIREN
Half woman and half bird, the sirens lured sailors to their deaths on the rocks of their island with their enchanting singing. Only Odysseus outwitted them; having himself bound to the mast of his ship he could hear them but wasincapable of heeding their call.

SOBEK
Egyptian crocodile-god with links to royalty arising from the concept of instant destruction for any enemy. His mother was the creator-goddess **Neith** of Sais. In Upper Egypt, at the temple complex of Kombo on the banks of the Nile, he was worshipped along with his wife, **Hathor**, and their child, **Khonsu**.

Silvanus (center), with two attendants.

A Siren.

The crocodile god Sobek.

SOKAR

Egyptian hawk-god worshipped in the Memphite necropoli. He amalgamated with the great creator-god to become "Ptah-Sokar." In Underworld, scenes Sokar became the "Lord of the Mysterious Region" and his head emerged from the sand mound over which the sun-god passed in a gesture of resurrection. His festival emphasized the resurrection of the god-king.

SPHINX

Ancient Egyptian mythic hybrid creature, with a human head and the body of a lion. Sphinxes were a manifestation of the sun-god. They were often positioned overlooking or near to necropoli (graveyards), and acted as guardians, especially of royalty and royal pyramids.

In Greek mythology the Sphinx was a monster sent by the goddess **Hera** to ravage Thebes; the monster was eventually destroyed by **Oedipus**.

The Sphinx uplit.

T

TAMMUZ

Babylonian equivalent of the Syrian fertility-god Atis, and the consort and brother of the earth and mother-goddess **Ishtar**. His annual death, resurrection, and marriage indicate a fertility ritual connected with the agricultural cycle. An Akkadian fragment describes the ritual wailing of Ishtar for Tammuz, and her descent into the Underworld.

Lady of the Horizon, Taweret.

TANTALUS

In Greek myth Tantalus was punished in **Hades** for impiety. The different reasons include: stealing the gods' nectar to give to mortal friends; revealing the gods' secrets; serving up the flesh of his own son, Pelops, to the gods; or stealing **Zeus**' guard dog on Crete. He was punished by being "tantalized:" hungry and thirsty, he was placed in front of a pool of water and fruit trees. Whenever he tried to reach either they shrank away.

Tantalus was the son of either Zeus or Troilus He was father of Pelops, and his descendants included Thyestes and the house of **Atreus**.

TARPEIA

The daughter of the governor of the citadel in Rome. Tempted by the gold of the Sabines' bracelets and collars, she allowed their army to enter the fortress, but was crushed to death by them. She was buried on the Capitoline Hill in Rome, giving her name to the Tarpeian Rock at its south-west corner.

TAWERET

Egyptian goddess who, despite being represented as a terrifying pregnant hippopotamus, was one of the most delightful and benign deities. She was the protectress of women in childbirth, and dangerous enough to ward off hostile threats at that crucial period. From this personal role Taweret is translated to a cosmic deity as "Lady of the Horizon," forming the constellation of the Hippopotamus as conceived by the Egyptians to exist in the northern sky.

TEFNUT

Egyptian goddesss personifying the moisture inherent in atmosphere. She and her brother-consort, **Shu**, were created from the semen or spittle of **Atum**. As a daughter of the sun-god, Tefnut became another "Eye of **Re**," and could take the form of a raging lioness.

TELEPHUS

In Greek myth the son of **Heracles** and Auge, and king of Mysia in Asia Minor. Several versions of his story exist; the most usual is that, after his birth on Mount Parthenon, he was abandoned at sea with his mother. They drifted to Mysia where he was brought up at court. A potentially incestuous marriage to his mother was prevented when a snake rose up between the two, allowing them time to recognize each other.

Telephus was wounded by **Achilles** when the Greeks landed in Mysia on their way to Troy. The Delphic oracle told him cryptically that the wounder would also heal him. Telephus helped the Greeks find their way eight years later when they returned, and as his reward Achilles agreed to heal him with the rust on his spear.

TESHUB

The characteristic god of Anatolia (as with Syria) is a weather god, depicted as driving in his chariot pulled by bulls. In the Hurrian pantheon, his wife was Hebat. Teshub's father was Kumarbi, and the *Song of Ullikumni* tells of a conspiracy launched by Kumarbi against Teshub, who had usurped his place as king of the gods. Kumarbi recruits the sea in the contest. The child Ullikumni is born in the sea, and set on the shoulders of Upelluri, who attains enormous size. Teshub uses an ancient knife to combat Ullikumni's magic diorite stone, and renders him powerless. This myth has been compared to the Greek myth of Typhon.

THESEUS

In Greek myth the national hero of Athens and Attica. He was the son of Aethra by either Aegeus, king of Athens, or **Poseidon**, who in some versions slept with Aethra on the same night that she slept with the childless Aegeus. At Athens he was seen as an ancestral king and founder of Athenian democracy. As a hero he was identified closely with **Heracles**, and he is said to have joined him and **Jason** in the Golden Fleece expedition and in the hunt for the Calydonian boar.

Theseus fighting the Minotaur.

Thoth in baboon mode.

He was brought up at Troezen. Before his birth, Aegeus had placed his sword and sandals under a heavy stone for his son to take at his manhood, which Theseus duly did. On his way to Athens he encountered and killed various enemies, and his father recognized him by the sword. Aegeus' wife, **Medea**, now made a unsuccessful bid to poison Theseus and maintain her position. She then set him a series of tasks designed to get rid of him, including killing the bull Heracles brought back from Crete. This he accomplished easily.

The next task was more difficult. The yearly tribute of seven boys and seven girls to the **Minotaur** was due, so Theseus went as part of it in order to destroy the Minotaur. **Ariadne**, the daughter of **Minos**, fell in love with him and helped him succeed. He took her back with him, but then abandoned her on Naxos. He then caused his father, Aegeus, to jump to his death because he had forgotten to change the black sails of his outward journey to white for a triumphant return.

As mythical king Theseus reorganized Attica as a confederacy of states, with Athens as its capital, and began to set up democracy. But he had to quell an Amazon invasion caused by his abduction of Queen **Hippolyta**.

Thoth in anthropomorphic form.

THOTH

In Egyptian mythology the vizier of the sun-god, with responsibility for scribal knowledge and science. His emblem was the moon and he could be represented as a baboon, but also, in anthropomorphic form, with the head of an Ibis—the earlier and more stately portrayal of the god.

The association of Thoth with scribes permeated Egyptian society. It was he who gave the knowledge of writing in hieroglyphics, which was always considered to be charged with a magical force. Because Thoth was impartial and unsusceptible to bribes, he was in charge of the scales weighing the hearts of the deceased in the Underworld, to see if their crimes were to severe for them to enter the realm of **Osiris**. He declared those who passed this test as "True of Voice" or justified.

U, V, W

URANUS

In Greek myth the son of **Gaia** (Earth) and also her husband. As the personification of Sky, Uranus was connected with the fertility of the earth; he covered it and by it had many children, including **Cronus**. But he hated his children and confined them to Tartarus, a part of the Underworld, as soon as they were born. Gaia was sick of continual childbearing, so she persuaded Cronus to castrate Uranus and dethrone him. The severed testicles, thrown into the sea, took root as an island; from the drops of blood sprang the race of giants; and from the sea-foam around his limbs **Aphrodite** sprang.

Venus.

UTANAPISHTIM

Also known as Ziusudra, Utanapishtim was a Sumerian king and flood hero, who appears in the Old Babylonian Sumerian Flood Story and is credited with saving mankind from destruction. He was rewarded with eternal life in the land of Dilmun. In a different Sumerian composition, *The Instructions of Shuruppak*, Ziusudra received the practical advice of living from his father, Shuruppak, in the form of short proverbial sayings.

In the Babylonica of Berrossus his name survives as Xisouthros in the Greek version of the mesopotamian flood story. Utanapishtim is his counterpart in the *Epic of **Gilgamesh***.

VENUS

The Roman goddess of love, associated from the second century BC with **Aphrodite**. Very little is known of the worship of Venus, but her cult began in pre-Roman Italy, where she was the deity of gardens and vegetation.

Venus was known as the daughter of **Jupiter** and Dione, but the better-known story is that she was born from sea-foam and wafted by the wind to Cyprus. Her son, **Cupid**, acted on her instructions to fire such individuals as **Psyche** with love

Venus de Milo.

The Temple of Vesta at Rome.

by the touch of his arrow. Venus also had a magic girdle that inspired love. She was the victim of her own schemes when she wounded herself with one of Cupid's arrows and the first man she saw was **Adonis**, for whom she developed an instant passion. Anxious not to lose him, she tried, but failed, to persuade him to stop hunting, and he was killed by a boar.

The name Venus means "beauty" or "charm," for which she was famed. The Julians—the family of Julius Caesar and the Emperor Augustus—claimed to be descended from **Aeneas**, a son of Venus by Anchises.

VESTA

One of the 10 great Roman deities and identified with the Greek Hestia, goddess of the hearth. Vesta was the guardian of Rome and while her sacred fire burned, Rome remained safe. The fire was allowed to go out on the first of March (New Year's day) and was then relit. If it went out at any other time, there were heavy penalties. The fire was tended by four Vestal Virgins, selected usually from patrician families, who served for 30 years and then returned to their home lives. The penalty for being unchaste was burial alive in an underground chamber. The festival of Vesta (the Vestalia) was celebrated on 9 June each year. This was a rest day for Vesta's sacred animal, the ass.

VULCAN

The Roman smith god, equivalent to the Greek **Hephaestus**. He was traditionally introduced to Rome by either **Romulus** or Titus Tatius. There are no specific legends concerning Vulcan, but he played an important part in the success of various heroes by providing invincible armor for them. In Virgil's *Aeneid,*

Wadjet.

Wepwawet.

Vulcan made a superb suit of armor for **Aeneas** at **Venus**' request. He made a shield (called the Aegis) and thunderbolts for **Jupiter** and in return received Venus as his wife.

At the Vulcanalia, his festival, little fish and other small animals were thrown into fires. These offerings represented human lives and were made to spare humans from death.

WADJET

Ancient Egyptian cobra-goddess of the Delta, and preserver of royal authority. Along with her southern counterpart, **Nekhbet**, she was an important part of the royal insignia, featuring as the *Uraeus* cobra in the Double Crown. Her cult centre was at Buto, also known as Pe. Wadjet is depicted as a cobra rearing up poised to strike. In her role as an "Eye of **Re**" she could be portrayed as a lioness.

WEPWAWET

Ancient Egyptian jackal deity from Upper Egypt, particularly the regions of Abydos and Assint. The name Wepwawet means "Opener of the Ways," which could be interpreted as a promulgator of royal conquests abroad. In a funerary context the adze of Wepwawet was one of the implements used to touch the royal ceremony of vivification known as "opening of the mouth." He also guided the deceased on a good path through the perils of the Underworld.

X, Y, Z

ZEUS

The supreme ruler of the Greek pantheon, son of **Cronus** who toppled his father and seized power. Zeus originally took control of the sky, but by the time of Homer he had become all-powerful, manifesting that power in storms though he was primarily concerned with justice.

Zeus intervened in all aspects of human and divine life. He assisted in the labors of **Heracles**, and intervened in the quarrel between Heracles and **Apollo** over the tripod at Delphi. In all things justice was done, although at times it seemed rather harsh and extreme.

Zeus.

His wife, **Hera**, was not alone in bearing his children, and although not literally the father of all the gods, he was connected with most of the demi-gods and heroes throughout Greek history.

Not surprisingly, his many affairs caused Hera some irritation, but Zeus was unaffected. His first wife had been Metis, who was the mother of **Athena**. Here he almost repeated his father's approach by swallowing Metis after Athena had been born to nullify the prediction that the second child, a son, would de-throne him. He then married Themis, and their children included Dike (Justice), Eunomia (Discipline), Eirene (Peace), and the Horae (Seasons). He was also father of the Fates, hence the different aspects of Zeus sprung from and were part of him.

Aphrodite was his daughter by Dione. Other important offspring were **Apollo** and **Artemis**. He then married Hera and had three children by her. Of his frequent affairs with mortals, many were carried out in the shape of a particular animal; **Europa** was taken by a bull, **Danae** by a shower of gold, and **Ganymede** by an eagle.

Zeus.

Credits

The publisher wishes to thank the following, who kindly supplied the photographs on the specified pages.

C. M. Dixon
3 (both), 5, 6/7, 11, 13, 14/15, 17, 18/19, 21, 22/23, 24, 26/27, 29, 31, 32, 33, 36, 37, 38, 40, 41, 45, 48, 50, 52, 56 (below), 57, 58, 59, 61, 64, 65, 70, 72, 75, 77, 79, 81, 82, 85, 86, 87, 88, 94, 101, 104, 106, 106, 107, 113, 114 (below), 115, 122, 123, 130, 131, 134, 136, 138, 143, 153, 154, 158, 159

Christie's Images
2 (both), 8, 9, 10, 12, 20, 35, 39, 43, 44, 51, 53, 54, 56 (top), 60, 62, 66, 67, 69, 76, 80, 83, 91, 95 (both), 96/97, 99, 100, 102, 103, 105, 108, 109, 111, 112/113, 114 (above), 116, 120, 124, 126, 127, 128, 129 (both), 135, 137, 140, 144, 145, 148, 149, 151, 152, 155, 156/157

A.N.T Photo-Library
16, 28, 47, 89, 92, 118, 133, 146, 150

Egyptian Tourist board
142, 147